Honoring God With My Body

ENDORSEMENTS FOR *HONORING GOD WITH MY BODY*

Honoring God with My Body is a wonderful new Bible study for those who have embarked on the journey of wellness. Author Katherine Pasour has done a fabulous job of blending Scriptural guidance and practical steps to encourage and equip you with everything you'll need to finish your race strong, healthy, and whole. It's nine weeks to a better you—spirit, mind, and body. I can't think of a better gift to give yourself. Whether you do this study by yourself or with a group, it's sure to be a blessing in your life.

—**Michelle Medlock Adams**, award-winning author of more than 100 books including *They Call Me Mom* and *Springtime for Your Spirit*

With so much focus on health and wellness in our world today, Katherine Pasour's book, *Honoring God With My Body*, has come in a perfect season. Get ready to study what God has to say about this amazing vessel He has given to us and to what both He and Katherine have to say about the best way to take care of it—all of it, body, soul, and spirit.

—**Eva Marie Everson**, President, Word Weavers International, Inc., Author of *The Third Path*

A healthy lifestyle equals freedom and Katherine has given us the key to living in this freedom...truth. Using scripture as a foundation, she gently walks the reader through attainable goals for lasting change. I wish I had *"Honoring God with My Body"* years ago!

—**Terri Broome**, Speaker, Blogger, Author of *The Ordinary Road*

After decades of teaching Bible studies and health and physical education classes, Katherine Pasour shares her knowledge and experiences to give the reader the most complete wellness Bible study out there! Covering the areas of physical, intellectual/mental, emotional, social, and vocational health, Pasour merges scriptural guidance with practical tips and suggestions to help the reader replace unhealthy habits with positive ones. Pasour takes the reader, step by step, on a journey to a healthier lifestyle that honors God from head to toe and on bended knee!

—**Julie Lavender**, author of *365 Ways to Love Your Child: Turning Little Moments into Lasting Memories* (Revell) and *Children's Bible Stories for Bedtime* (Zeitgeist/Penguin Random House)

Katherine Pasour guides us, not only to healthy choices, but to exploring dimensions of spiritual, physical, emotional, and vocational health. In *Honoring God with My Body*, she weaves her expertise in nutrition and Bible study with kindness, practicality, and Scripture to promote lifestyle change. Dr. Pasour reminds us of God's lavish love for us, His delight in our wellness, and how we can better serve Him.

—**Marilyn Nutter**, Author (with April White), *Destination Hope: A Travel Companion WhenLife Falls Apart*

In *Honoring God with My Body*, Katherine writes with enthusiasm and sound biblical wisdom. While this is an excellent individual resource for learning about God's design for our bodies, participants who use it in group study will experience success through shared struggles and accountability.

—**Mary A Felkins**, M.S. in Nutrition; Author of *Call to Love, You Are the Reason* and *What the Morning Brings: 52 Inspirational Story-Style Devotions*

In *Honoring God with My Body*, Katherine Pasour feeds our souls with Scripture and gives us insights into God's perspective on our health and lives. She encourages us to lay down not-so-good habits and pick up the ones that will make us stronger and healthier for God's purpose for our lives.

It would be a joy to go through this book with a group. The discussion questions will help us to hear from others that we're not alone in the struggle to eat right, exercise, and be as healthy as possible. Groups can discuss the Bible verses and apply them to daily life. Katherine suggests that a discussion group could enjoy walking together and share a snack before they discuss each chapter—that sounds like health for the body and the soul.

—**Katy Kauffman**, magazine editor and
award-winning Bible study author

Our bodies are the Temple of the Holy Spirit—as a result, God has given us every good food to take care of it. In *Honoring God with My Body*, Katherine explains how healthy food choices and physical exercise can help us enjoy good health. She also reveals that health is more than just physical: our health is "mental/intellectual, emotional, social, vocational, and spiritual." Balance is crucial.

Katherine challenges us to be "Fit for Service" and a "Light for Jesus." God has called us to use our gifts and talents for His glory.

But, most importantly, Katherine shares that the love of God through His Son, Jesus, is everything we need. The Creator of all things loves, cherishes, and has chosen us. We can do all things through Christ—especially living and eating well.

—**Stephanie Pavlantos**, author of *Jewels of Hebrews*;
Biologist, and Bible teacher

HONORING GOD
with My Body

Journey to Wellness
and a Healthy Lifestyle

KATHERINE PASOUR

NASHVILLE

NEW YORK • LONDON • MELBOURNE • VANCOUVER

Honoring God With My Body
Journey to Wellness and a Healthy Lifestyle

© 2023 Katherine Pasour

Published in New York, New York, by Morgan James Publishing. Morgan James is a trademark of Morgan James, LLC. www.MorganJamesPublishing.com

Proudly distributed by Ingram Publisher Services.

Morgan James BOGO™

A **FREE** ebook edition is available for you or a friend with the purchase of this print book.

CLEARLY SIGN YOUR NAME ABOVE

Instructions to claim your free ebook edition:
1. Visit MorganJamesBOGO.com
2. Sign your name CLEARLY in the space above
3. Complete the form and submit a photo of this entire page
4. You or your friend can download the ebook to your preferred device

ISBN 9781631958731 paperback
ISBN 9781631958748 ebook
Library of Congress Control Number:
2021953184

Cover & Interior Design by:
Christopher Kirk
www.GFSstudio.com

Morgan James is a proud partner of Habitat for Humanity Peninsula and Greater Williamsburg. Partners in building since 2006.

Get involved today! Visit MorganJamesPublishing.com/giving-back

TABLE OF CONTENTS

ACKNOWLEDGMENTS

For everyone who has faced the challenge of overcoming certain lifestyle choices that contribute to poor health, we know how difficult breaking bad habits and establishing healthy new choices can be. This book began in my own struggles to achieve wellness and progressed into a study to help others.

For my husband, Bob, who is always my best role model for service to others, this book would not have been possible without your encouragement and your support of my continuing education, my career as a teacher, and my vocation as a servant of God.

To my siblings and children, who served as sounding boards for ideas and as proofreaders and who loved me despite the weirdness and quirkiness that goes with being a writer.

To my church family—you have been with me through the hard times, continued to love me, and prayed for me. A special thank you to my dear friends, Carolyn Anderson, for being the world's greatest encourager and Debbie Booker for loving me across the miles.

To my colleagues at Lenoir-Rhyne University, thank you for the opportunity to teach and serve in the College of Health Science. My years with you and the students of LR allowed me to grow in knowledge, faith, and confidence to serve others.

To my Lighthouse Bible Studies family who understands the challenges of being an author; who love, encourage, and support each other on social media and at conferences; and who exemplify the grace, faith, and love of Jesus in your daily lives.

To Morgan James Publishing who believed in me and the impact this book could have on the lives of those striving for better health. Thank you, Terry Whalin, for your enthusiasm and encouragement. Thank you, David Hancock, for reaching out in support of a new author. Thank you, Heidi Nickerson and the entire Morgan James' team, for assisting and supporting me in the publishing process.

For my editor, Aubrey Kosa, I am grateful for your cheerfulness, dependability, encouragement, and skill in helping my book be the best it can be.

For all who struggle with the goal of achieving and maintaining wellness through healthier lifestyle choices, I understand your struggle, and my thoughts and prayers are with you on your journey.

WEEK ONE:

Introduction

Goals for Week One

1. Meet and learn about those joining us on our journey to wellness.
2. Recognize that we are awesome and amazing Creations from God.
3. Affirm that Jesus sent us a Counselor—the Holy Spirit— to dwell within us.
4. Study the similarities between our body and a symphony of praise.
5. Emphasize the Holy Bible as our guide toward wellness.
6. Review the organization of our study.

OUR BODY IS A TEMPLE
OF THE HOLY SPIRIT

Do you not know that your body is a temple of the Holy Spirit, who is in you, whom you have received from God? You are not your own; you were bought at a price. Therefore honor God with your body.

1 Corinthians 6:19–20

In Paul's letter to the Corinthians, as he reminded his readers that the Holy Spirit dwelled within them, he cautioned them against sexual immorality. However, the apostle also emphasized to the Corinthians—and to us—the vital importance of honoring God with our body. We are urged to care for all aspects of health for our bodies. Keeping our temple—the home of the Holy Spirit—in a healthy condition honors our Creator.

As Jesus was preparing to leave his disciples, he promised them a Comforter and Counselor:

"If you love me, you will obey what I command. And I will ask the Father, and he will give you another Counselor to be with

you forever—the Spirit of truth. The world cannot accept him,
because it neither sees him nor knows him. But you know
him, for he lives with you and will be in you. I will not leave
you as orphans; I will come to you. Before long, the world
will not see me anymore, but you will see me. Because I live,
you also will live. On that day you will realize that I am in my
Father, and you are in me, and I am in you. Whoever has my
commands and obeys them, he is the one who loves me. He
who loves me will be loved by my Father, and I too will love
him and show myself to him."

John 14:15–21

Jesus loved his disciples so much that he didn't leave them alone
when it was time for him to go to the Father. That applies to us as well.
We are not alone; we have the Holy Spirit. Because we are God's children,
saved by grace through the sacrifice of our Lord Jesus, we have a divine
being living within us. How awesome is that? Shouldn't we honor that
gift by making our temple (our body) as healthy as possible to house the
Holy Spirit?

This Bible study, *Honoring God with My Body,* prayerfully and scrip-
turally guides us to healthier lifestyle choices that will improve our health.
The study is designed for those affirming or seeking wellness so that they
might better serve their Lord.

Wellness refers to our quality of life and includes all dimensions of
health. There are multiple aspects of good health, but our study will focus
on the following six: spiritual, physical, emotional, intellectual, social,
and vocational. The study goes into more detail on each of these in later
sections, but as an introduction to this theme, it's important to remember that all aspects of health are interdependent. When one dimension
suffers (such as when we are physically in poor health, under extreme
stress, or emotionally depressed), all aspects of our health are affected. To

be all that God intended us to be, and to have the wellbeing to live to our fullest in service to Him, we need to be healthy in *all* aspects of wellness.

Consider an orchestra performing a symphony—the composer authors an awesome musical creation; the orchestra works together in balance and harmony, practicing faithfully to achieve their best performance; the conductor mentors, guides, and directs the entire process; and the subsequent performance brings excitement, joy, and appreciation to those blessed to hear it.

Let's imagine our body as that awesome creation from God. If we focus on all dimensions of health, bringing the aspects together in balance (a condition of equilibrium) and harmony (agreement, peace, melodious sound), our body can achieve wellness.[1] Jesus (our spiritual guide) is our conductor for every aspect of our lives. In uniting all the dimensions of wellness to reach our fullest potential for good health, we honor God by providing a healthy dwelling place for the Holy Spirit.

It is good to praise the LORD and make music to your name, O Most High, proclaiming your love in the morning and your faithfulness at night, to the music of the ten-stringed lyre and the melody of the harp. For you make me glad by your deeds, LORD; I sing with joy at what your hands have done. How great are your works, LORD, how profound your thoughts!
Psalm 92:1–5

SING TO THE LORD
A NEW SONG

Music, both vocal and instrumental, has expressed human emotion since ancient times. The Israelites were no exception to this practice—"all of life could be brought under the spell of song."[2] And we see in the Bible that music and dancing were used in times of celebration.

> Why did you run off secretly and deceive me? Why didn't you tell me, so I could send you away with joy and singing to the music of timbrels and harps?
> ### *Genesis 31:27*

Jesus also tells of a father who rejoiced at the return of his son, whom he believed had been lost to him forever.

> "Meanwhile the older son was in the field. When he came to the house, he heard music and dancing."
> ### *Luke 15:25*

The people of Israel celebrated in the streets at David's success in defeating the Philistines.

> When the men were returning home after David had killed the Philistine, the women came out from all the towns of Israel to meet King Saul with singing and dancing, with joyful songs and with timbrels and lyres.
>
> *1 Samuel 18:6*

Can our bodies be a joyous symphony in praise and glory to God? Our Lord, our Creator, bestowed this vessel upon us—our body—as a dwelling place for the Holy Spirit. With balance and harmony, the many dimensions of health can come together into a symphony of beautiful music with Jesus as our conductor.

> Sing to the LORD a new song, for he has done marvelous things; his right hand and his holy arm have worked salvation for him.
> The LORD has made his salvation known and revealed his righteousness to the nations.
> He has remembered his love and his faithfulness to Israel; all the ends of the earth have seen the salvation of our God.
> Shout for joy to the LORD, all the earth, burst into jubilant song with music; make music to the LORD with the harp, with the harp and the sound of singing, with trumpets and the blast of the ram's horn—shout for joy before the LORD, the King.
>
> *Psalm 98:1–6*

THE BIBLE IS OUR GUIDE

The Bible provides us with powerful insights to guide us on our journey toward wellness. According to Howard Stone and James O. Duke in *How to Think Theologically*, "scripture is both a historical record of God's people and the early Christians" and "a message from God—the Word of God."[3] Thus, as we seek guidance from the Bible, studying the "Word of God," we discover insight into many issues that directly affect our health as God's Word supports us to seek the pathway to a healthier lifestyle.

Reading the Bible also helps us understand the meaning of our faith, but we must be careful of "proof-texting" (picking and choosing specific scripture to support one's own views); it is important to look at the message of the Bible *as a whole*.[4]

Love is a major theme throughout the Bible—God's love for His people, His call for His people to love and worship Him, the gift of sacrifice and grace shared by Jesus because of His great love for us, and our commandment to love one another. We love our families, and our families love us, and we want to be as healthy as we can for them. We are called to serve God and witness for Jesus, and we can better do that task if we are as healthy as God meant for us to be. We are commanded to "love one another" (John 13:34–35), and we can more easily accomplish that task if we are in good health.

Honoring God with My Body is about love. Throughout our study together, you will acquire knowledge to help you make healthier lifestyle choices. We know that God loves us with a powerful and everlasting love. That love will guide us as we seek to improve our health—to honor God with a healthy temple to house the Holy Spirit.

Each of us is in a different stage of our walk of faith, as well as our journey toward wellness, but I pray you will join me on the overarching pathway to better health.

ORGANIZATION OF OUR STUDY

This Bible study's themes are divided into weekly topics with consistent emphasis on wellness. I warn you, there is homework! I pray you will complete the daily readings, answer brief questions, and complete your weekly reflections. Your participation during the week will enable you to pray for each other and prepare you for the weekly meetings during which further information is shared.

You can complete the Bible study individually or with a partner; however, meeting with a group offers you additional support as you work toward developing healthier habits. Within the group setting, your leader will highlight important points from the week's readings, guide discussions with questions and reflective responses, and provide additional information to encourage healthy lifestyle choices. Participants are encouraged to pray for each other during the week, and weekly group meetings provide additional opportunities for members of the group to offer support to each other.

If you have questions for me, my contact information is at the end of this book. I'll be praying for you!

Wishing you blessings on your journey to wellness,

Katherine

WEEK TWO:

God Loves You

Goals for Week Two

1. Remember that God created us and considered this aspect of His creation to be **"very good."**
2. Recognize God loves us and has a plan for our lives (which includes being healthy).
3. Examine the barriers we face on the road to good health.
4. Discuss the importance of fruits and vegetables (and eating more of them).
5. Look at our past doubts and fears—identify them, hash them out (if needed), give them to God, and *move on*!

GOD, OUR CREATOR, LOVES US

In the book of Genesis, God's process of creating our Earth and human beings (us!) is described.

On the first day, God created light:

God saw that the light was good, and he separated the light from the darkness.
Genesis 1:4

On the second day, God created the sky:

And God said, "Let there be a vault between the waters to separate water from water." ... God called the vault "sky."
Genesis 1:6, 8

On the third day, God gathered the water to certain areas so that dry land would appear:

God called the dry ground "land," and the gathered waters he called "seas." And God saw that it was good.

Genesis 1:10

And he created plants:

The land produced vegetation ... And God saw that it was good.

Genesis 1:12

On the fourth day, God made two great lights:

God set them in the vault of the sky to give light on the earth, to govern the day and the night, and to separate light from darkness. And God saw that it was good.

Genesis 1:17–18

On the fifth day God created creatures of the sea, birds, and animals on land:

So God created the great creatures of the sea and every living thing with which the water teems ... and every winged bird ... and God saw that it was good.

Genesis 1:21

God made the wild animals ... the livestock ... and all creatures that move along the ground ... and God saw that it was good.

Genesis 1:25

But, on the sixth day:

So God created mankind in his own image, in the image of God he created them; male and female he created them.

Genesis 1:27

God saw all that he had made, and it was very good.

Genesis 1:31

Each day of God's Creation, *it was good*, but on the sixth day, when God created humans, *it was very good*.

We have only to look around at God's Creation to know how amazing and awesome the Earth is, yet when humans were created, it was *very good!* We are very special to God.

DAY 1

"For I know the plans I have for you," declares the Lord, "plans to prosper you and not to harm you, plans to give you hope and a future. Then you will call upon me and come and pray to me, and I will listen to you. You will seek me and find me when you seek me with all your heart."
Jeremiah 29:11–13

Both the Old and the New Testament Christian Bible are filled with references of God's great love for us. Perhaps the greatest example of this love is the gift of His Son. Jesus said to Nicodemus:

"For God so loved the world that he gave his one and only Son, that whoever believes in him shall not perish but have eternal life. For God did not send his Son into the world to condemn the world, but to save the world through him."
John 3:16–17

But despite being told numerous times that God loves us, don't we still have doubts and fears? Don't we profess belief in God's love for all people, but sometimes wonder if He is really concerned about our day-to-day lives?

What is one problem or concern in your life that you label as too trivial for God to worry about?

_____

_____

_____

_____

_____

Please read Psalm 18:16–19.

Isn't it amazing to know that God delights in us?

I know that, like mine, your blessings are too numerous to count, but take a moment to list at least five things you are thankful for.

_____

_____

_____

_____

_____

Our Prayer: Father, it is so wonderful to know that you delight in me. It humbles me to know but fills me with great joy. I pray for everyone in this Bible study—that you will guide us to better health, so we might better serve you.

DAY 2

Jesus prepared His disciples before sending them out to witness. One of the messages he shared was of the Father's great love for them.

> "Are not two sparrows sold for a penny? Yet not one of them will fall to the ground apart from the will of your Father. And even the very hairs of your head are all numbered. So don't be afraid; you are worth more than many sparrows."
> *Matthew 10:29–31*

The good news is that God loves us, just as He loved the disciples. It's also wonderful that God knows us—every aspect of our lives—*and* loves us anyway! Yet it can be terrifying to realize that God knows everything about us—all the down and dirty, our secrets, our sins, our jealousy and covetousness, our bad habits, and more. God knows it all. But that's okay, because that gives us the freedom to turn everything over to God and seek His guidance in making changes that will help us on our road toward wellness.

In this Bible study, we're not going to share all our deep, dark secrets. We don't need to know each other that well! However, since this is a journey toward wellness, it is time for you to examine some of the barriers you face on your path to better health.

We'll talk in the weekly meeting about heredity (what we get from our parents) and environmental influences (the choices we make that affect our health). Some aspects of our health are beyond our control, but other choices we make have a serious impact on our health. We're not planning to solve these issues today (we will work on them later), but the first step is to identify our health issues, bad habits, and health-risk behaviors that negatively impact our wellness.

So, be brave and list a few things you do that you know are not good for you.

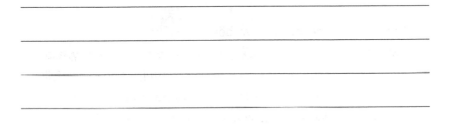

Our Prayer: Father, I pray for the courage to recognize unhealthy behaviors and habits that are keeping me from embracing life to the fullest. As we all seek the journey to better health, we pray for your strength, guidance, and encouragement.

DAY 3

Please read Psalm 139 in its entirety.
Now let's review verses 13–16.

For you created my inmost being; you knit me together in my mother's womb. I praise you because I am fearfully and wonderfully made; your works are wonderful, I know that full well. My frame was not hidden from you when I was made in the secret place. When I was woven together in the depths of the earth, your eyes saw my unformed body. All the days ordained for me were written in your book before one of them came to be.

When we think about the human body, we recognize that we truly are "**fearfully and wonderfully made**." It's so amazing that we can see, hear, smell, taste, touch, move, think, speak, love—we can do so many awesome things! We are God's most treasured creation.

Please read Genesis 1:27–30. In these verses, we are reminded that we are created in the image of God, that God has given humankind dominion over the world, and that God gifted humankind with "every green plant for food."

Meat eaters are probably worrying, "Oh, no! She's going to try to turn me into a vegetarian or a vegan." Don't worry, the Bible doesn't suggest that we should never eat meat; however, God is obviously giving us the message that food from plants is good. We will discuss the importance of fruits and vegetables (and the way they are prepared) in the group meeting. For now, please list some fruits and vegetables you enjoy.

_____

_____

_____

_____

_____

Nutritionists recommend we eat at least five servings of fruits and vegetables (prepared in a healthy way) every day. For the next few days (until the group meeting), please keep a log of how many servings of fruits and vegetables you eat each day. A serving is half a cup, a medium-sized piece of fruit (apple, banana, etc.), or one cup of fresh, leafy greens (like lettuce or spinach). Fresh or frozen are healthier choices, followed by steamed (if cooking is desired). Try to avoid canned produce because of the high sodium content. Butter, salt, sugar, rich sauces, or frying can negatively affect the nutritional quality of food.

Our Prayer: As your creation, we are blessed in so many ways. We pray for guidance and perseverance in our quest to eat healthier fruits and vegetables, your gifts to us.

DAY 4

And hope does not disappoint us, because God has poured out his love into our hearts by the Holy Spirit, whom he has given us.

Romans 5:5

We all carry around doubts and fears—baggage from past failures.

Perhaps we attempted to take steps toward better health in the past (dieting, an exercise program, cutting out sodas, etc.), but we failed. We've been unsuccessful in changing bad habits and accepted that we're just going to live with our state of health. Or worse, we haven't recognized how those bad habits can be deadly.

Please bear with me as I share some statistics you may not want to hear.

- Chronic disease is the leading cause of death and disability in the United States.
- Heart disease and cancer account for 48 percent of all deaths.
- Obesity is a serious concern in the United States and contributes significantly to the development of chronic diseases such as heart disease, diabetes, and cancer.[5]

Chronic disease can be caused by health-risk behaviors, and heredity is also a contributing factor. Health-risk behaviors are those we can change. Examples are:

- Poor nutrition
- Lack of regular physical activity
- Tobacco and alcohol use

We'll go into more detail about specific health-risk behaviors later in our study.

Now let's think about that baggage we may be carrying around that might lead us into some of these dangerous choices. Are you practicing any of the following risky behaviors: unhealthy eating, lack of exercise, smoking, etc.? You may want to journal about this on a separate page or on the reflection page at the end of this week. I encourage you to examine your feelings, dig deep for root causes, write them down, give them to God, pray for guidance, and most importantly, don't pick up the burden again!

_____

_____

_____

_____

_____

Our Prayer: Father, we know we are created in your image—that you love us and want us to be healthy, not only to be in service to You but also to live a life of joy.

DAY 5

Yesterday may have been a tough day for you after I asked you to examine the baggage you carry around—things that have occurred in your life that have dragged you down and contributed to picking up bad habits that negatively affect your health. I'm praying for you! We're praying for each other!

Paul wrote in his letter to the Ephesians:

I keep asking that the God of our Lord Jesus Christ, the glorious Father, may give you the Spirit of wisdom and revelation, so that you may know him better. I pray also that the eyes of your heart may be enlightened in order that you may know the hope to which he has called you, the riches of his glorious inheritance in the saints, and his incomparably great power for us who believe. That power is like the working of his mighty strength, which he exerted in Christ when he raised him from the dead and seated him at his right hand in the heavenly realms, far above all rule and authority, power and dominion, and every title that can be given, not only in the present age but also in the one to come. And God placed

all things under his feet and appointed him to be head over everything for the church, which is his body, the fullness of him who fills everything in every way.
Ephesians 1:17–23

This letter is so rich with blessing and praise. And the most wonderful thing is that it applies to us—now! Biblical wisdom speaks to us and for us, just as it did when originally written. We can be assured that as God's people (the church), we are under the care of Jesus (looking again at that last verse). We are part of the body of Christ. He lives in us!

Let us care for our temple (our body) in which our Lord resides. Eat your fruits and vegetables!

Prayer: Father, I pray for each member of our group—that we can bring our burdens to you, leave them there, and accept your strength and encouragement to guide us on our journey toward better health.

REFLECTIONS ON WEEK TWO: GOD LOVES YOU

How does knowing about God's great love for you make you feel?

_____

_____

_____

_____

_____

On Day 2, you listed some of your unhealthy behaviors. Have you thought of any more you wish to admit?

_____

_____

_____

_____

_____

If you wish, journal about the burdens you carry around. Write a letter to God describing those burdens and lay them at His feet. He doesn't promise to remove our trials, but he will be with us on our journey.

_____

_____

_____

_____

_____

Have you been able to add fruits and vegetables to your daily meals? Are they eaten fresh or prepared with minimal fat and salt?

_____

_____

_____

_____

WEEK THREE:

Loving Ourselves and Others

Goals for Week Three:

1. Recognize and be thankful for the awesome gifts of our loving God.
2. Continue to affirm God's love for us.
3. Pray for each other on the journey toward healthier lifestyle choices.
4. Identify challenges and stressors in our lives.
5. Select one lifestyle change to make that will contribute to a healthier you.

GOD DOES NOT
MAKE JUNK

Last week we focused on God's amazing Creation—not just the Universe, the Earth, but *us*! When God made us, it was **very good**. We are **"fearfully and wonderfully made,"** and God *loves* us.

What is our response to this awesome gift?

Give thanks to the Lord, for he is good; his love endures forever. Let the redeemed of the LORD tell their story—those he redeemed from the hand of the foe, those he gathered from the lands, from east and west, from north and south. Some wandered in desert wastelands, finding no way to a city where they could settle. They were hungry and thirsty, and their lives ebbed away. Then they cried out to the LORD in their trouble, and he delivered them from their distress. He led them by a straight way to a city where they could settle. Let them give thanks to the LORD for his unfailing love and his wonderful deeds for mankind, for he satisfies the thirsty and fills the hungry with good things.

Psalm 107:1–9

Remember the saying "God don't make no junk"? Please pardon my grammar; the phrase really gets the point across. Because God created us in His image, because he loves us so much that He sent His Son as a Holy and living sacrifice, because he gifted us with an amazing brain and body (and we are physically blessed in numerous other ways), because He cares for us through the trials of life, and because He doesn't give up on us when we sin, our response is to be thankful. We love, praise, and worship God.

We should also recognize that as God's amazing creation, we should love and respect both ourselves and others. I'm not recommending that we be self-centered and boastful, but we need to love ourselves to care for our body that houses the Holy Spirit. We also must feel good about (love) ourselves if we are going to be able to love one another (our spouse, children, family, friends, church family, coworkers, and even strangers) and bring peace and harmony to our lives, our community, and our world.

Jesus replied: "'Love the Lord your God with all your heart and with all your soul and with all your mind.' This is the first and greatest commandment. And the second is like it: 'Love your neighbor as yourself.' All the Law and the Prophets hang on these two commandments."
Matthew 22:38–40

DAY 1

Dear friends, since God so loved us, we also ought to love one another. No one has ever seen God; but if we love one another, God lives in us and his love is made complete in us.
1 John 4:11–12

We know that God loves us—the Bible tells us! Remember the children's song "Jesus Loves Me"? I hope we never get too old to sing it.

*Jesus loves **ME** [and you], this I **KNOW**;*
For the Bible tells me so.
(bold formatting and bracketed words added)

Please continue to read 1 John 4:13 through 1 John 5:5. List five important messages John is sharing with us.

1. _____

2. _____

3. _____

4. _____

5. _____

Did you notice "**everyone born of God overcomes the world**"? Our relationship with Jesus allows us to overcome the temptations the world places in front of us on a daily (or even hourly) basis.

What were some challenges that you faced this week?

_____

_____

_____

_____

_____

Our Prayer: Father, we know You love us because the Bible tells us so! You love us and that enables us to love ourselves and each other. Through Your love, You give us strength and courage to overcome the temptations of the world. Help us to encourage one another on our journey to a closer relationship with You. I pray for each of my sisters and brothers in Christ as we strive to make healthier lifestyle choices.

DAY 2

How do we know that Jesus cares about our challenges and our suffering? How do we know that He wants us to be as healthy as possible?

Chronic diseases are conditions lasting one year or more and/or require ongoing medical attention or limit our daily activities.[6] Poor health and chronic disease can imprison us, robbing us of our opportunity to live life to the fullest. The development of obesity, diabetes, heart disease, or substance abuse limits our ability to live an abundant life.

When Jesus began His ministry after His time in the wilderness, one of His first public appearances was in Nazareth. The Gospel of Luke describes what happened when Jesus went to the synagogue on the Sabbath.

The scroll of the prophet Isaiah was handed to him. Unrolling it, he found the place where it is written: "The Spirit of the Lord is on me, because he has anointed me to preach good news to the poor, He has sent me to proclaim freedom for the prisoner and recovery of sight for the blind, to release the oppressed, to proclaim the year of the Lord's favor. Then he rolled up the scroll, gave it back to the attendant and sat down. The eyes of everyone in the synagogue were fastened on him, and he began by saying to them, "Today this scripture is fulfilled in your hearing."

Luke 4:17–21

That just gives me cold chills—to think about being in the presence of our Lord and hearing Him read those words. What about you?

How comforting to know that He came not only to save us from our sins but to free us from oppression, blindness (in all its forms), and captivity.

What's holding you in captivity at this moment?

_____

_____

_____

_____

_____

Our Prayer: Father, we're all doing some soul searching. Help us to be open and honest with You and with ourselves.

DAY 3

Above all, love each other deeply, because love covers over
a multitude of sins.

1 Peter 4:8

This may be a challenging day for you as we continue to address chronic
disease. Remember, I'm praying for you. Please pray for each other.

The Cost of Poor Health

Chronic diseases (heart disease, stroke, diabetes, obesity, cancer, substance abuse) are among the most costly and preventable health conditions. Heart disease, cancer, and diabetes alone cost more than $3.8
trillion in annual healthcare costs.[7]

Chronic diseases are the leading cause of death and disability in the
United States. In 2018, six in ten adults had a chronic health condition
that negatively affected their lives and four in ten adults had two or more
chronic diseases.[8]

Obesity is considered a serious health concern—more than 40 percent of adults are obese.[9] Diabetes is the leading cause of kidney failure,
lower-limb amputations (excluding accidents), and new cases of blind-

ness in adults. In addition, 90 percent of Americans consume too much sodium, increasing their risk of high blood pressure (a contributor to heart disease).

Here's the key point: many chronic diseases (although not all) can be prevented! Our lifestyle choices (risky behaviors or healthy choices) can have a strong impact on whether we develop chronic diseases. By maintaining a healthy lifestyle, we reduce that risk. Furthermore, changing negative habits can reduce the severity of chronic diseases already present.

Prayer: Father, we know many adults suffer from chronic diseases that limit their ability to live the abundant life you planned for us. Please help us to recognize and reduce risky behaviors that contribute to the development of chronic diseases.

DAY 4

As a prisoner of the Lord, then I urge you to live a life worthy
of the calling you have received. Be completely humble and
gentle; be patient bearing with one another in love. Make
every effort to keep the unity of the Spirit through the bond
of peace.
Ephesians 4:1–3

Earlier this week (and last week as well), I asked you to do some soul
searching about what is holding you in captivity. Many things can keep
us in bondage. Examples could include unresolved resentment or anger,
jealousy, bitterness, or unforgiveness.

Get rid of all bitterness, rage, and anger, brawling and slander,
along with every form of malice. Be kind and compassionate
to one another, forgiving each other, just as in Christ God
forgave you.
Ephesians 4:31–32

What are some things that cause stress or anxiety in your life?

38

_____

_____

_____

_____

_____

Getting rid of some of those things may be easier said than done. We might have issues from our childhood or adult life that bind us. If our past or present situation is preventing us from living life to the fullest, then those issues hold us in captivity, and if this bondage contributes to us engaging in behaviors that lead us to risk our health, then those concerns must be addressed. We can't live a joyful life as a child of God if we are being controlled by risky lifestyle choices that threaten our health.

I encourage you to journal about any past issues that still affect your health today. There's space to do so on the reflection page at the end of this week or feel free to use a separate journal. I'm praying for you!

Our Prayer: Father, there are some things that I would rather not look back on and think about, yet I know some of those issues are creating problems for my health now and I need to recognize these burdens I'm still carrying around. I need to put a name to these issues and give them to You. I pray for my brothers and sisters; please guide us to recognize painful memories one more time before we leave the burden at Your altar.

DAY 5

Let us hold unswervingly to the hope we profess, for he who promised is faithful. And let us consider how we may spur one another on toward love and good deeds.
Hebrews 10:23–24

Today will be another hard day, but I hope and pray you will persevere.

After praying for guidance, please list five of your habits or lifestyle choices you believe might be unhealthy for you. You can choose to share all of these in the group meeting if you wish, but you can also keep them confidential if you prefer.

1. _____

2. _____

3. _____

4. _____

5. _____

We're not going to attempt to solve everything at once. Please prayerfully consider one of these to share with the group at this week's group meeting. We want to pray for you. Throughout the remaining weeks in our study, we'll discuss strategies to implement new habits and choices that will be healthier.

What action would you like to work on first?

_____

_____

_____

_____

_____

Our Prayer: Father, this has been a tough week. I've had to examine myself closely and look at ingrained habits that are harmful for me. There are some things I don't want to give up! Please help us make wise choices that will guide us to better health. I pray for each member of our group as we identify a habit that's threatening our body—our temple of the Holy Spirit. There are some things we need to change. Please guide us on our journey.

REFLECTIONS ON WEEK THREE: LOVING OURSELVES AND OTHERS

Your brothers and sisters in Christ have been praying for you this week. We share the knowledge that Jesus loves us and we love each other. Has that made the examination of your health habits easier?

_____

_____

_____

_____

_____

Are you limited by any chronic diseases? Although heredity and unknown causes also factor into the development of chronic diseases, how have your habits and behaviors contributed to your condition(s)?

_____

_____

_____

_____

_____

I encourage you to write a letter to God, pouring out all your past pain, anger, bitterness, and burdens. Give it all to God. He is big enough to carry the burden. Give it to Him and *let it go*!

_____

_____

_____

_____

Please continue to pray for your friends in our Bible study. It shows your love for them as they attempt to make healthy changes. As Paul wrote to the Romans:

Let no debt remain outstanding, except the continuing debt to love one another, for whoever loves others has fulfilled the law.
Romans 13:8

WEEK FOUR:

Jesus Walked

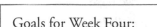

Goals for Week Four:

1. Learn about health-related fitness and how our body benefits from being physically fit.
2. Discuss what exercises are valuable for us and how to begin an exercise program.*
3. Based on the FITT-VP Principle, learn how hard we should exercise and how to determine intensity.
4. Develop strategies for adding physical activity to our daily lives.
5. Continue to pray for each other.

*If you are not currently involved in a regular exercise program or have one or more chronic health conditions, you should check with your healthcare provider before beginning an exercise program.

THE BENEFITS
OF PHYSICAL ACTIVITY

Our bodies were created to be physically active; we have 206 bones and over 600 muscles that are "fearfully and wonderfully" stitched together in an amazing way that allows us to walk, run, jump, climb, balance, stretch, lift objects, dance, play games, clean our house, mow grass, and much more. While most of us will never be Olympic athletes or professional basketball players, we can all achieve health-related physical fitness, which greatly benefits our wellbeing.

So, what does the Bible tell us about exercise? Not a lot.

> For physical training is of some value, but godliness has value
> for all things, holding promise for both the present life and the
> life to come.
> ### *1 Timothy 5:4*

We must keep in mind, however, that most people during the time in which the scriptures were written led an active lifestyle. The primary mode of transportation on land was walking. There was little mechani-

46

zation, and for the majority, survival depended upon hard physical labor. Few had the luxury of leisure time.

Now there were athletes during this time period. The ancient Olympics began in 776 B.C. and continued for twelve centuries. There was also war, and soldiers were in physical training for increasing their strength and skill. So the authors of the New Testament were familiar with physical exercise for making the body stronger. Paul the Apostle, gifted in the use of metaphor (figurative language that uses one thing to describe or represent another), uses the imagery of a race to emphasize the need for self-discipline in our journey with Christ.

> Do you not know that in a race all the runners run, but only one gets the prize? Run in such a way as to get the prize. Everyone who competes in the games goes into strict training. They do it to get a crown that will not last, but we do it to get a crown that will last forever. Therefore I do not run like someone running aimlessly; I do not fight like a boxer beating the air. No, I strike a blow to my body and make it my slave so that after I have preached to others, I myself will not be disqualified for the prize.
>
> *1 Corinthians 9:24–27*

Our relationship with Jesus Christ is the most important aspect of our lives, but keeping our temple (our body) healthy to house the Holy Spirit is vital as well. As Paul says, let's make our body our slave. Thus, with scripture as our guide, we can be in charge of our journey toward wellness.

Regular physical activity is an essential aspect of achieving and maintaining our temple as a suitable dwelling for the Holy Spirit.

DAY 1

As Jesus was walking beside the Sea of Galilee, he saw two
brothers, Simon called Peter and his brother Andrew.
Matthew 4:18a

During the three years of His ministry, Jesus traveled extensively through-
out Judea, Samaria, and Galilee. Walking was the primary mode of travel.
While Jerusalem and Bethany are fairly close to each other, Nazareth and
Galilee are more than fifty miles from Jerusalem, and Caesarea Philippi,
and Tyre are more than one hundred miles north of Jerusalem. Jesus and
His disciples walked a lot!

According to the Centers for Disease Control, few lifestyle changes
have as much power to positively impact your health as physical activity.
The benefits of health-related physical fitness include:

- Strengthening the heart muscle
- Strengthening bones and muscles
- Reducing the likelihood of developing heart disease
- Reducing the risk of diabetes
- Reducing the risk of some cancers

- Helping maintain healthier weight
- Improving mental health/reducing stress
- Reducing risk of osteoporosis
- Reducing level of brain cell loss and helping prevent Alzheimer's disease
- Improving balance and reducing risk of falling for older adults
- Helping us live longer with a better quality of life

Wow—look at this list—exercise is good for us! So why isn't everyone working to achieve physical fitness if exercise is a miracle cure? What do you think?

_____

_____

_____

_____

_____

Our Prayer: Father, I pray You will open our minds and hearts to learn about health-related physical fitness, help us to recognize the benefits of achieving and maintaining health-related fitness, and guide us to be motivated to be more physically active.

DAY 2

Once again Jesus went out beside the lake. A large crowd came to him, and he began to teach them. As he walked along, he saw Levi ...

Mark 2:13–14a

Being physically active can lead us to achieving health-related fitness, but it's important for us to know what this means.

There are five components to health-related physical fitness. We'll discuss two of those today *and* how to achieve fitness in those two components.

The first component is cardiorespiratory endurance, and it is directly related to the health and strength of your heart muscle. It is the ability of your heart and lungs to work efficiently together to perform sustained physical work. Good cardiorespiratory endurance is the component of physical fitness most correlated to longevity (living longer). Individuals with good cardiorespiratory endurance are more likely to live longer lives with a better quality of life.

We achieve better cardiorespiratory endurance by working our heart muscle harder than it's normally accustomed to (remember, you should check with your healthcare provider before beginning an exercise program). Activities that strengthen our heart include walking briskly, running, swimming, aerobics, cycling, jumping rope, dancing, stair climbing, etc.—basically any activity that gets our heart rate up to a training level and keeps it up benefits our heart. We'll talk about how to know your training level in this week's group meeting.

So, how hard should we work/exercise? In general, you should work hard enough to breathe faster and work up a sweat, but you should still be able to carry on a conversation. One recommendation is to work hard enough so that you can't sing but can still speak.

Another component of health-related physical fitness is body composition: the relationship of lean body mass to body fat. We improve our body composition with regular physical activity and healthy nutrition. Having a healthy body composition greatly reduces our risk of obesity, heart disease, and diabetes.

One of the greatest benefits of health-related physical fitness is being able to perform our daily activities better (walking, lifting, household and yard work, etc.).

DAY 3

One Sabbath Jesus was going through the grain fields, and
as his disciples walked along, they began to pick some heads
of grain.

Mark 2:23

In addition to cardiorespiratory endurance and body composition, there
are three other components of health-related fitness.

The first of these is muscular strength, which is the maximum contractile ability of your muscle in a single contraction. In terms relevant
to most of us, this refers to our ability to lift heavy objects. Weight lifters
obviously strive for this type of fitness, but ordinary people also need
muscular strength to complete our daily activities, such as carrying groceries, moving furniture, and lifting children and grandchildren.

Muscular endurance, on the other hand, is the ability of our muscles
to perform sustained work. Cardiorespiratory endurance is specific to the
heart muscle while muscular endurance refers to all other muscles. If we
were to decide to climb all the steps of the Washington Monument, we
would need good cardiorespiratory endurance because that much exer-

cise needs a strong heart, but we would also need good muscular endurance in our legs to be able to climb all those steps.

The last component we'll review is flexibility—range of motion, our ability to stretch. We need flexibility to accomplish our daily activities like bending, reaching, and exercising. Flexibility is also important for maintaining good balance, which helps prevent falls.

We can improve our muscular strength and endurance through resistance training (adding weight or resistance to exercise). Resistance training can be accomplished in the weight room, using resistance bands, or doing exercises such as push-ups, crunches, squats, and lunges that use our own body weight as the resistance. Likewise, we improve our flexibility by stretching.

We'll review safe exercise guidelines in this week's group meeting.

Our Prayer: Father, all this information on improving our personal fitness is confusing. I pray You will guide us to greater understanding and be with us on our journey to improving our fitness. We want to honor our temple of the Holy Spirit.

DAY 4

Then came the Feast of Dedication at Jerusalem. It was winter, and Jesus was in the temple area walking in Solomon's Colonnade.

John 10:23

Walking is one of the best exercises we can do to improve health-related fitness. Walking doesn't require any equipment except a good pair of shoes (a necessity). If you aren't already walking regularly, you should start gradually in both length and frequency. Your goal should be to eventually walk for thirty to sixty minutes five times a week (150 or more minutes a week). Your walking doesn't have to be all at once. For example, ten minutes, three times a day still counts as thirty minutes. And if you are able (you may need to work up to it), your walk should be brisk, not a stroll.

If you have not been active and are just starting a walking program, a possible progression is listed below.

- Week 1: five minutes, three times a day, three days per week
- Week 2: ten minutes, three times a day, three days per week

54

- Week 3: ten minutes, three times a day, four days per week
- Week 4: fifteen minutes, twice a day, four days per week
- Week 5: thirty minutes, once a day, four times per week
- Week 6: thirty minutes (or more), once a day, five times per week

This is just a suggested progression. Feel free to vary according to your abilities and time. Just keep in mind that you are working toward the goal of at least 150 minutes per week, thirty minutes a day, five days a week.

If you are already physically active, you will progress faster, but don't push too hard at first so that you don't get discouraged. Find a buddy to walk with so that you can encourage each other. If walking is not your chosen method to work on cardiorespiratory endurance, just be sure to have another regular physical activity that strengthens your heart.

Remember to pray and encourage each other!

DAY 5

*As they talked and discussed these things with each other,
Jesus himself came up and walked along with them ...*
Luke 24:15a

As we learned at the beginning of this week, Jesus walked a *lot*. The distances between the towns and cities to which Jesus traveled were significant. This active lifestyle would have helped Jesus and His disciples maintain healthy weights. Europeans and Asians tend to walk and bicycle more than Americans. Part of that may be because things are so spread out in the United States (we're a big country), but the overall result includes less active lifestyles and Americans becoming big as the numbers of overweight and obese children and adults continue to increase.

Below are strategies for adding more walking to your life.

- When possible, walk or cycle rather than using motorized transportation.
- When a car is necessary, park farther away from your destination to add some exercise.

- Take the stairs rather than an elevator or escalator (or walk up the escalator).
- If working in a sedentary job, take a walking break often.
- When watching television or working on the computer, take frequent breaks for a short walk (this not only will help your heart but also your back, neck, and eyes). You can also place some light weights or a resistance band near your favorite television spot to remind you to exercise during commercials, or you can set a timer for exercise breaks.
- Find a buddy who will walk with you and make a date to walk three to five days a week. If the weather is bad outside, you can meet at church, the mall, or a large building to walk.

Alright, it's confession time: what has been holding you back from increasing your physical activity? What is one way you can increase your physical activity to work toward a healthier heart?

_____

_____

_____

_____

_____

Our Prayer: Father, the Bible tells us that Jesus walked a lot. As Your Son, I can't imagine anyone being more attentive to caring for the earthly body You provided for Him while on Earth. I pray that You will help me and everyone in our group to walk more and be more physically active so that we, too, can honor this earthly body that has been Your gift to us.

REFLECTIONS ON WEEK FOUR: JESUS WALKED

Please think a little more about the barriers that may be preventing you from having an active lifestyle. Perhaps you weren't aware of the importance of physical activity (remember, on Day 1 of this week we reviewed how being physically fit can help you have a healthier heart, maintain a healthy weight, and help you live a longer, healthier life). Perhaps you know that you should be active, but somehow a sedentary lifestyle just snuck up on you. If you wish, list some of the reasons that you aren't physically active enough for good health.

_____

_____

_____

_____

_____

Now that you've examined some of the reasons that you aren't as active as you should be for good health, consider what small changes you can make to add more physical activity to your week. List some of the possibilities here. If you feel like sharing, please do so in this week's group meeting to provide ideas for others.

_____

_____

_____

_____

Which of these ideas would you like to start doing this upcoming week? Do you have a buddy to exercise with who will help encourage you?

_____

_____

_____

_____

Remember to pray for your group (and for yourself)!

FITT-VP Principle

F—Frequency (how often you should exercise—three to five days a week)

I—Intensity (how hard you work—enough to get the heart rate up and breathe harder)

T—Time (how long you should exercise—the goal is to build up to a total of thirty to sixty minutes a day)

T—Type (the type of exercise you choose will be affected by your goals and your preferences)

V—Variety (we may become bored with the same routine; varying your routine can help prevent boredom and increase motivation)

P—Progression (as your body becomes accustomed to exercise, you can add more time, intensity, or distance to continue to improve health-related fitness).

WEEK FIVE:

Never Give Up

Goals for Week Five:

1. Recognize that Satan does not want us to succeed in our goal to have a stronger relationship with God or to have a healthy body to house the temple of the Holy Spirit.
2. Immerse ourselves into God's Word as a powerful tool to keep us from giving in to the devil's schemes.
3. Actively support and encourage each other to maintain a healthy lifestyle, thus defeating Satan.
4. Recognize that God *loves* us, even though we aren't perfect!

DON'T GIVE UP!

> *"Never give in. Never give in. Never, never, never, never—in nothing great or small, large or petty—never give in, except to conditions of honor and good sense. Never yield to force. Never yield to apparently overwhelming might of the enemy."*
> Winston Churchill

We've all struggled to "do the right thing." Often those tough decisions refer to a moral or legal issue. Sometimes those decisions or actions may be relatively small (going five miles over the speed limit) or much bigger (spreading gossip). In the worst-case scenarios, people make bad choices that bring great harm to themselves and/or others (driving while impaired).

Paul writes about his struggle to "do the right thing" in his letter to the Romans.

We know that the law is spiritual, but I am unspiritual, sold as a slave to sin. I do not understand what I do. For what I want to do I do not do, but what I hate, I do. And if I do what I do not want to do, I agree that the law is good. As it is, it is no longer I myself who do it, but it is sin living in me. For I know that good itself does not dwell in me, that is, in my sinful nature. For I have the desire to do what is good, but I cannot carry it out. For I do not do the good I want to do, but the evil I do not want to do—this I keep doing. Now if I do what I do not want to do, it is no longer I who do it, but it is sin living in me that does it.

Romans 7:14–20

Remember, Jesus promised us a Comforter and a Counselor, the Spirit of Truth (John 14:15–21). The Holy Spirit will guide us to resist the temptations thrown into our path. When the devil tells us that we cannot succeed in making positive lifestyle changes, we can turn to the Holy Spirit for strength.

Those who live according to the flesh have their minds set on what the flesh desires; but those who live in accordance with the Spirit have their minds set on what the Spirit desires. The mind governed by the flesh is death, but the mind governed by the Spirit is life and peace ... Those who are in the realm of the flesh cannot please God. You, however, are not in the realm of the flesh but are in the realm of the Spirit, if indeed the Spirit lives within you.

Romans 8:5–6, 8–9

Believers, Christ lives within you! What an awesome and amazing gift we have received. He will guide you to be strong—to resist the temptations of the flesh—and He will lead you on your journey to wellness. The Holy Spirit will help us to persevere and overcome our weakness.

In the same way, the Spirit helps us in our weakness. We do not know what we ought to pray for, but the Spirit himself intercedes for us through wordless groans.

Romans 8:26

Persevere on your journey to wellness. Never give up!

DAY 1

Let us not become weary in doing good, for at the proper time
we will reap a harvest if we do not give up.
Galatians 6:9

When we try to make changes in our lives to draw closer to God, the devil doesn't like it and will try to place roadblocks. Satan will tell us that we will fail; he'll tell us that we don't have the self-discipline to make changes in our lifestyle and that God doesn't care about whether we are healthy or what we eat or if we exercise. Satan will tell us that our health is "good enough," so why bother to go to all the trouble of making those "hard" changes?

Counselor Roger Alliman writes, "The battle is between God and righteousness on the one side and Satan and sin on the other. God's vehicles are the person of the Holy Spirit and truth. Satan's vehicles are sin, deception, temptation, and doubt."[10] The devil wants us to doubt our relationship with Jesus. He wants us to be uncertain about God's love for us. The devil wants us to fail because if Satan can separate us from Christ (by convincing us that Jesus doesn't care about our health), Satan wins.

What doubts has the devil put into your mind during the past four weeks?

_____

_____

_____

_____

_____

What barriers has he erected to separate you from God?

_____

_____

_____

_____

_____

What has made you believe that you cannot make healthy lifestyle changes?

_____

_____

_____

_____

_____

Remember, Christ wants us to have "abundant life," and a healthy life is very abundant indeed. So, like Winston Churchill says, "Never give in!" Don't let the devil win. Fight for your healthy life.

In Week Two, I asked you to select one action or change that you could make that would be a healthy choice for you. Have you made progress on that goal?

_____

_____

_____

_____

_____

I'm praying for you! And I believe *you* can take steps toward a healthier life.

DAY 2

The Lord does not look at the things people look at. People look at the outward appearance, but the Lord looks at the heart.
1 Samuel 16:7b

The devil tempts us with worldly issues. Television, social media, and pictures at the checkout line in the supermarket bombard us with images of the perfect man or woman. Our brains tell us these images are unrealistic, but the constant visual reminders attempt to persuade us that we are less worthy if we don't dress a certain way, have designer clothes, and drive a new car. Even as we label social demands as consumerism or advertising gimmicks, don't we sometimes wish for those material things?

Or we mess up—we make a mistake at work, we argue with our spouse or children, we hurt our friend's feelings. Who is there, waiting to remind us of our imperfection? Satan, of course, is eager to point out our faults because he thrives on our discouragement, our doubts, and our failures.

How does the devil know all our weaknesses?

The Lord said to Satan, "Where have you come from?" Satan answered, "From roaming throughout the earth, going back and forth on it."

Job 1:7

The devil is busy. He's looking for a foothold (see Ephesians 4:27). But we have God on our side.

No temptation has overtaken you except what is common to mankind. And God is faithful; he will not let you be tempted beyond what you can bear. But when you are tempted, he will also provide a way out so that you can endure it.

1 Corinthians 10:13

Being in God's Word and praying are important weapons for us to resist the temptations of the world and the power of sin. Please read Ephesians 6:10–17 and pray for encouragement for our entire group.

DAY 3

Am I now trying to win the approval of human beings, or of God? Or am I trying to please people? If I were still trying to please people, I would not be a servant of Christ.
Galatians 1:10

Have I not commanded you? Be strong and courageous. Do not be afraid; do not be discouraged, for the Lord your God will be with you wherever you go.
Joshua 1:9

If you're like me, sometimes you need an encouraging word. When we're trying to give up bad habits or start healthy (but challenging) new habits, we *definitely* need hopeful and helpful feedback. Have you prayed for your friends in this Bible study today? If not, now is a good time!

Jesus replied, "Truly I tell you, if you have faith and do not doubt, not only can you do what was done to the fig tree, but also you can say to this mountain, 'Go throw yourself into

the sea,' and it will be done. If you believe, you will receive
whatever you ask for in prayer."
Matthew 21:21–22

Believe! Have *faith*! I hope you won't cause any trees to wither, but I
pray you will believe and have faith that you can succeed in eliminating
some harmful and unhealthy behaviors and begin new habits that will
help you along the path toward wellness. I also pray that you will believe
and have faith that your friends in this Bible study will also succeed on
their journey toward wellness. Please encourage them!

What has encouraged you today?

_____

_____

_____

_____

_____

*Our Prayer: Father, sometimes I get very discouraged, but when I read of Your
faithfulness to Your people in Your Word, I am encouraged to persevere on my
journey toward wellness. But this journey is hard. We do not have the strength
on our own to resist the devil's schemes. Please be with us as we continue to
work toward a healthy body to serve as a temple for the Holy Spirit.*

DAY 4

May the Lord answer you when you are in distress; may the
name of the God of Jacob protect you.
May he send you help from the sanctuary and grant you
support from Zion.
May he remember all your sacrifices and accept your burnt
offerings.
May he give you the desires of your heart and make all your
plans succeed.
Psalm 20:1–4

Sometimes we must be courageous enough to ask for help. Often, we feel
that we need to make a journey alone—that it is weak to seek help—but
that is not so! It takes courage to admit that we cannot do something alone.

When you are feeling discouraged (and you will, as we all do sometimes), please, *please*, ask for help.

Talk to God.

Pray.

Be in God's Word.

And ask your Bible study support group to help!

Sometimes it feels like our family doesn't always support us when we're trying to make positive lifestyle changes. Unintentionally, our family and friends sometimes even hinder our efforts to make healthy choices. You may not feel comfortable bringing this to your family's attention, but take a moment now to jot down any concerns about the support you're receiving from family and friends. You can choose to share them during this week's group meeting if you wish, and it may help just to voice your concerns on paper. There will also be an opportunity during the group meeting to discuss strategies that might help your friends and family be more supportive.

_____

_____

_____

_____

_____

I always thank my God as I remember you in my prayers, because I hear about your love for all his holy people and your faith in the Lord Jesus. I pray that your partnership with us in the faith may be effective in deepening your understanding of every good thing that we share for the sake of Christ.
Philemon 1:4–6

DAY 5

So whether you eat or drink or whatever you do, do it all for the glory of God.

1 Corinthians 10:13

It's been another tough week, but there's victory in Jesus! Paul writes to the Ephesians:

You were taught, with regard to your former way of life, to put off your old self, which is being corrupted by deceitful desires; to be made new in the attitude of your minds; and to put on the new self, created to be like God in true righteousness and holiness.

Ephesians 4:22–24

Paul is writing, of course, about putting away our old life of sin and being reborn in Jesus. However, we can apply this concept to putting away the bad habits that hinder our ability to serve our God to our fullest potential. Remember, our body is a temple of the Holy Spirit; keeping that temple healthy and strong for the Holy Spirit is important.

Therefore, if anyone is in Christ, the new creation has come:
The old has gone, the new is here!
2 Corinthians 5:17

Now as you continue to "put away" some of those unhealthy habits, I ask you to choose one additional lifestyle behavior to change (either working to eliminate an unhealthy behavior or adding a new, healthy change). Please write that goal down either here, in a separate journal, or on this week's reflection page.

_____

_____

_____

_____

_____

On this week's reflection page, please list some strategies you can use to begin to make this change.

Our Prayer: This week, Father, we delved deeply into Your Word to seek encouraging scripture to protect us from the devil and encourage us on our journey. We are so grateful for Your love, faithfulness, and protection. We are a new Creation in Christ because He lives in us. Please continue to guide us on our journey toward wellness so that our temple will be a healthy dwelling place for Jesus.

REFLECTIONS ON WEEK FIVE: NEVER GIVE UP

This week has featured several scriptures focusing on faith, encouragement, and perseverance. Please select one that was especially meaningful for you and write it here. I encourage you to read it aloud.

_____

_____

_____

_____

_____

Time for a progress report. What was your first goal from Week Two (a lifestyle change or new habit you wanted to begin)? Please briefly discuss your first goal: Are you making progress? What have been the greatest challenges you have faced in attempting to make these changes? How can your Bible study group encourage you? Do you need to revise this goal?

_____

_____

_____

_____

_____

On Day 5 of this week, I asked you to choose another lifestyle change to make (either eliminate an unhealthy behavior or add a healthy change). Please write this new goal and list several strategies you plan to use to achieve it. If you are willing to share in this week's group meeting, the group can offer support and perhaps some additional strategies to help you get off to a good start.

_____

_____

_____

_____

Since this is check-up week, please list your physical activity for this week. Have you gradually increased your walking?

_____

_____

_____

_____

I'm praying for each of you, dear friends, that you will recognize how much *God loves you* and how much He wants you to succeed on this journey toward wellness.

WEEK SIX:

Feeding the Temple

Goals for Week Six

1. Review the six nutrients (carbohydrates, protein, fat, water, vitamins, minerals) our bodies need every day.
2. Recognize the importance of eating a balanced diet, emphasizing fruits and vegetables, whole grains, lean meats, low-fat dairy, and limited fat (all prepared in a healthy way).
3. Learn about portion sizes.
4. Recognize the importance of reading food labels and being selective in choosing healthy foods.
5. Recognize the importance of fiber in our daily diet.
6. Recognize the dangers of overweight and obesity.
7. Discuss how to shop for and choose healthy food.

WE ARE WHAT WE EAT

They will eat the fruit of their ways and be filled with the fruit of their schemes.

Proverbs 1:31

The emphasis of this week's study is nutrition. I call this week's focus "Feeding the Temple," but I also add the caveat that "We Are What We Eat."

"We Are What We Eat" is true both physically and spiritually. You've heard the saying, "Once on the lips, forever on the hips!" It's funny (and sad) but true. Our body is a reflection of the food we put into it (we can see this in the mirror). If we make healthy choices—eat lots of fruits and veggies; be careful to keep our intake of fat, sugar, and sodium within the healthy range; select low-fat and lean proteins; and avoid junk, fast, and processed foods—our body will be nutritionally healthy. However, if our diet choices include an excess of high-fat, sugary, and other unhealthy foods, our lack of health-related fitness—and our scales—may alert us to those unwise choices.

Now, Jesus provides our spiritual food.

Then Jesus declared, "I am the bread of life. Whoever comes to me will never go hungry, and whoever believes in me will never be thirsty ... I am the living bread that came down from heaven. Whoever eats this bread will live forever. This bread is my flesh, which I will give for the life of the world."

John 6:35, 51

The word *fruit* is used multiple times in the Bible—literally, figuratively, and metaphorically. The Greek word, *karpos*, translates literally as *fruit* or *offspring* but is used figuratively to mean "bearing fruit in the heart."[11]

Can we keep our temple of the Holy Spirit healthy so that we may bear spiritual fruit?

Jesus said, "By their fruit you will recognize them. Do people pick grapes from thornbushes, or figs from thistles? Likewise, every good tree bears good fruit, but a bad tree bears bad fruit."

Matthew 7:16–17

"I am the vine; you are the branches. If you remain in me and I in you, you will bear much fruit; apart from me you can do nothing."

John 15:5

For you were once darkness, but now you are light in the Lord. Live as children of light (for the fruit of the light consists in all goodness, righteousness and truth).

Ephesians 5:8–9

As we prepare ourselves to examine the food that we are putting into our temple for the Holy Spirit this week, shouldn't we also ask ourselves what type of "fruit" our actions reveal to the world?

DAY 1

The land produced: plants bearing seed according to their
kinds and trees bearing fruit with seed in it according to their
kinds. And God saw that it was good.
Genesis 1:12

Then God said, "I give you every seed-bearing plant on the
face of the whole earth and every tree that has fruit with seed
in it. They will be yours for food."
Genesis 1:29

Please read the first chapter of the book of Daniel.

Daniel believed that the food and wine provided by the officials of King Nebuchadnezzar would defile him, so he requested to eat vegetables and drink water instead. After ten days, Daniel and his friends "**looked healthier and better nourished than any of the young men who ate the royal food**" (Daniel 1:15).

The Hebrew word that translates to vegetables means "things sown" and likely included anything that grows from seeds. Daniel ate a plant-based diet of grains, vegetables, and fruit (We'll discuss the benefits of a plant-based diet in this week's group meeting).

So, what are the advantages of fruits and vegetables? They are loaded with complex carbohydrates, vitamins, minerals, and fiber (the good stuff!) and are filling (to help keep us from eating too much of the less healthy stuff). Eating plenty of fruits and veggies can help prevent heart disease, high blood pressure, and some cancers. Especially good for you are dark, leafy, green vegetables (broccoli, spinach, collards, etc.), brightly colored vegetables (bell peppers, sweet potatoes, tomatoes, beets, etc.), all kinds of beans, and the tremendous variety of fruits. And there's more! Vegetables and fruits contain phytochemicals (antioxidants) that strengthen our immune system; reduce risk of heart disease, stroke, diabetes, and cancer; improve vision; lower cholesterol; and improve joint health.

Our Prayer: Father, we're getting into the tough stuff. This is hard! Food tastes great and is good for us, but sometimes we don't make the right choices. Help us to recognize that we must make wise decisions about what we eat to have a healthy body to be our temple for Your Holy Spirit.

DAY 2

Better a small serving of vegetables with love than a fattened
calf with hatred.
Proverbs 15:17

Dr. Oz makes the following recommendations for people's food choices:

- Avoid sugar and refined grains (white flour is an example of a refined grain).
- Load up on fresh vegetables, fruits, and lentils.
- Use protein as the side dish—not the main part of your meal.
- Eat healthy protein (fish, poultry, and whole grains).
- Work on healthy eating as a family or group so that you have support.[12]

What vegetables do you already like and eat regularly? What are some new ones you are willing to try? In the Additional Resources section, I list several resources for learning more about nutrition, the Daniel diet, and the importance of eating fruits and vegetables.

Keep in mind that the way we prepare vegetables and fruits makes a *big* difference in their health benefits. Eating them fresh is always best. The next best choice after fresh is frozen. Canned vegetables tend to be very high in sodium. Try to avoid high-calorie dressings on salads (there is always the choice of oil and vinegar or low-fat alternatives). Limit rich sauces (like cheese sauce on broccoli), the addition of butter and salt, and eating high-calorie dips (there are ways to reduce the fat and calories in dips and dressings). Fresh fruit is best, but if you buy canned, choose fruit that is packed in water or unsweetened juice rather than heavy syrup. Be careful of fruit juices because many brands contain added sugar.

Our Prayer: Father, we are learning, but there's so much to remember—what to eat, how much to eat, how to fix it, how to cut back on fats and sugar. Oh, my! We need Your help!

DAY 3

"But blessed is the one who trusts in the Lord, whose confidence is in him. They will be like a tree planted by the water that sends out its roots by the stream. It does not fear when heat comes; its leaves are always green. It has no worries in a year of drought and never fails to bear fruit."
Jeremiah 17:7–8

Are we confident that we can make the changes toward a healthier lifestyle? If you're like me, you're worried that you'll fail. The Bible tells us that God loves us and wants to bless us, Jesus came to give us more abundant life, and God loves us so much that He sent Jesus as a holy and living sacrifice. We have been given so many blessings! We can have complete confidence that God wants us to have the best health possible; therefore, He wants us to succeed on our journey toward wellness.

The Lord gives strength to his people; the Lord blesses his people with peace.
Psalm 29:11

Now, let's talk about a good habit that's not going to be too difficult to change: eating more fiber!

Fiber has many benefits for our body. It keeps our gut healthy so that we have good bowel habits and bowel health, lowers cholesterol, helps control blood sugar, and helps us achieve and maintain a healthy weight.

We get fiber from:

- Fruits and vegetables
- Whole-grain products
- Beans, peas, and other legumes
- Nuts and seeds

We'll talk in this week's group meeting about the amount of fiber you need and discuss ways to add fiber to your diet. (You will also find more information about fiber in Appendix D).

Our Prayer: Father, You have blessed us with so many wonderful foods that are good for us! I pray You will be with us as we learn to try new and healthy foods and try to cut back on those that are not healthy for us.

DAY 4

When David came to Mahanaim, Shobi son of Nahash from Rabbah of the Ammonites, and Makir son of Ammiel from Lo Debar, and Barzillai the Gileadite from Rogelim brought bedding and bowls and articles of pottery. They also brought wheat and barley, flour and roasted grain, beans, and lentils ...
2 Samuel 17:27–28

I will praise you as long as I live, and in your name I will lift up my hands. I will be satisfied as with the richest of foods.
Psalm 63:4–5

The people of ancient Israel, as well as those who lived during the same time as Jesus, consumed healthy foods: whole grains, beans, lentils, vegetables, fruits, olive oil, etc. They also had an active lifestyle. We can learn much from them—not only their love for their God and their faithfulness and obedience in worship but also their consumption of many plant-based foods.

How we prepare our food makes a tremendous difference in whether our food is healthy. As discussed earlier this week, fresh vegetables and fruits are the best choices, with frozen being the second-best option. If we cook our fresh or frozen vegetables, we should limit the amount of salt, butter, or other unhealthy additives. WebMD recommends that we consume no more than 2,300 mg of sodium per day, and the American Heart Association recommends no more than 1,500 mg of sodium per day. Canned vegetables are very high in sodium. To help us limit the amount of sodium we add to food, we can use herbs, lemon juice, and other low-sodium options to season our food.

Frying also drastically changes the healthiness of our food. For example, a medium-sized baked potato has 220 calories and 1 gram of fat. If we take that same potato and turn it into french fries, it has 700 calories and 34 grams of fat. Wow! Besides being loaded with calories, fried foods are more likely to cause acid reflux and irritable bowel syndrome (IBS).

What are your favorite fried foods? Can you reduce your intake of those fried foods?

_____

_____

_____

_____

_____

DAY 5

Food is used as a metaphor (figurative language or a phrase used to describe something to create a vivid comparison) in many instances in the Bible. Please read Luke 8:1–15. In those verses, Jesus uses the powerful imagery of seeds growing into a crop to make his point about the Word of God taking root in believers.

Likewise, Paul uses "fruit" symbolically in numerous instances.

We continually ask God to fill you with the knowledge of his will through all the wisdom and understanding that the spirit gives, so that you may live a life worthy of the Lord and please him in every way: bearing fruit in every good work, growing in the knowledge of God.

Colossians 1:9b–10

But the fruit of the Spirit is love, joy, peace, forbearance, kindness, goodness, faithfulness, gentleness and self-control. Against such things there is no law.

Galatians 5:22–23

God has presented us with the bounty of His creation. He created us with a need for food and the taste buds to enjoy eating. He also provided us with a multitude of choices. That multitude of choices sometimes creates a dilemma when we eat the wrong kinds of food or when we eat too much. Remember, though, God wants us to be healthy and free from disease. He also gave us free will, so we can choose to make healthier choices with His strength to guide us.

If you are currently struggling with making healthy food choices, please take a moment to reflect on what you believe are your barriers to eating a healthier diet. What's holding you back from healthy eating?

Our Prayer: Father, we have learned a lot this week about making healthier choices, but it's still hard! I pray You will be with us on this journey. As Jesus reminds us, "Man (or woman) does not live by bread alone, but on every word that comes from the mouth of God" (Matthew 4:4).

REFLECTIONS ON WEEK SIX: FEEDING THE TEMPLE

We've talked again this week about the importance of fruits and vegetables in your diet. Please take a few minutes to reflect on how you did with adding more fruits and veggies this week.

_____

_____

_____

_____

_____

This is the first week in our Bible study we've really focused on our eating habits. Please take a few moments to list five positive characteristics of your eating habits (i.e., five things you do that are healthy for you).

_____

_____

_____

_____

_____

Now the hard part—please list five things (related to your eating habits) that could lead to a healthier you if you were to change them (this could mean adding a positive action or working to eliminate a negative one). Can you select one of those and make a commitment to change starting now?

_____

_____

_____

_____

_____

Complete an update on your physical activity—have you been able to add walking and additional physical activity four or five days a week?

_____

_____

_____

_____

_____

WEEK SEVEN:

The Dimensions of Health

Goals for Week Seven

1. Recognize that there are numerous dimensions of health and that they are all interrelated.
2. Reflect on the physical, mental/intellectual, emotional, social, vocational, and spiritual aspects of health.
3. Check on our progress (without knocking ourselves down).
4. Continue to focus on healthy nutrition.

FINDING BALANCE AND HARMONY IN HEALTH

When all aspects of health effectively work together within our body, we become like that orchestra we discuss in the introduction to our Bible study. God our Creator (Composer) knitted us together "**fearfully and wonderfully**," and it was "**very good**." Jesus is our conductor, our mentor, and our guide so that we may live a life full of joy in service to him. With practice, work, and perseverance, *we* are that orchestra, creating the symphony of life.

If we focus on multiple dimensions of health, bringing them together in balance and harmony, our body can achieve wellness. This week, we will briefly study six dimensions of health. These are listed below and discussed in greater detail during your daily reading this week. One of our primary goals for our Bible study is to unite and balance all these aspects of wellness, so we can honor God by providing a healthy dwelling place for the Holy Spirit.

Below, short scriptural references emphasize each dimension. This is by no means the extent of the Bible's wisdom that can be applied to our health. I encourage you to seek the enormous amount of knowledge, insight, and encouragement found in the Bible during your daily

Bible reading. I pray you will apply God's wisdom to your daily journey toward wellness.

A BRIEF INTRODUCTION TO THE DIMENSIONS OF HEALTH

Physical

Our physical body is impacted (either positively or negatively) by all that we do: our nutrition, our daily activity levels, our healthcare plan, our mental and emotional wellbeing, etc. Scripture reminds us that God's people are conscious of the health of their physical bodies.

> At the end of ten days they looked healthier and better nourished than any of the young men who ate the royal food. So the guard took away their choice food and wine they were to drink and gave them vegetables instead.
> **Daniel 1:15–16**

Mental/Intellectual

Human intelligence is not emphasized strongly in the Bible except from the standpoint of the directive to use our intelligence, mental capabilities, and gifts in service to our Lord. Our knowledge or wisdom cannot compare to God's.

> For it is written: "I will destroy the wisdom of the wise; the intelligence of the intelligent I will frustrate." Where is the wise person? Where is the teacher of the law? Where is the philosopher of this age? Has not God made foolish the wisdom of the world?
>
> ***1 Corinthians 1:19–20***

However, we should seek God's wisdom as we work toward wellness because He will guide us to attain the necessary knowledge to make healthy choices. Our Father will also strengthen and encourage us on our journey to achieve wellness.

Emotional

God gives us the joy of love and happiness, but we also can feel sadness and deep emotional pain. Jesus and his disciples experienced the gamut of emotions, just as we do.

> Jesus saw that they wanted to ask him about this, so he said to them, "Are you asking one another what I meant when I said, 'In a little while you will see me no more, and then after a little while you will see me'? Very truly I tell you, you will weep and mourn while the world rejoices. You will grieve, but your grief will turn to joy.
>
> ***John 16:19–20***

At times, humans also experience depression and mental anguish.

> Whenever the spirit from God came on Saul, David would take up his lyre and play. Then relief would come to Saul; he would feel better, and the evil spirit would leave him.
>
> ***1 Samuel 16:23***

Social

We are reminded that, as God's people, we are to love one another, be kind and forgiving to one another, and work together to accomplish God's work on Earth.

> So in everything, do to others what you would have them do to you, for this sums up the Law and the Prophets.
> *Matthew 7:12*

> You, my brothers and sisters, were called to be free. But do not use your freedom to indulge the flesh, rather, serve one another humbly in love. For the entire law is fulfilled in keeping this one command: "Love your neighbor as yourself."
> *Galatians 5:13–14*

> Remind the people to be subject to rulers and authorities, to be obedient, to be ready to do whatever is good, to slander no one, to be peaceable and considerate, and always to be gentle toward everyone.
> *Titus 3:1–2*

> "In your anger do not sin." Do not let the sun go down while you are still angry and do not give the devil a foothold.
> *Ephesians 4:26–27*

Vocational

Vocational health is more than safety in the workplace; it can also refer to our calling, our purpose, our service, and our work toward making this world a better place for everyone.

> As a prisoner for the LORD, then, I urge you to live a life worthy of the calling you have received.
> ### Ephesians 4:1

> And whatever you do, whether in word or deed, do it all in the name of the Lord Jesus, giving thanks to God the Father through him.
> ### Colossians 3:17

Spiritual

Our path to a spiritual relationship with our Father is through His Son and our Savior, Jesus.

> Jesus answered, I am the way and the truth and the life. No one comes to the Father except through me.
> ### John 14:6

The Greek word, *hodos*, refers to *road* or *way*. It is used both literally and figuratively in the Bible.[13] In this case, we are reminded that Jesus is the only way—the only road to take on this spiritual journey of life. He can also be our strength and guide on our journey toward wellness.

Finding Balance in Our Health

How do we balance all the dimensions of health? We start by seeking God's wisdom.

> Be very careful, then, how you live—not as unwise but as wise, making the most of every opportunity, because the days are evil. Therefore do not be foolish, but understand what the Lord's will is.
> ### *Ephesians 5:15–17*

There is one more essential ingredient in achieving balance and wellness through the dimensions of health—discipline!

Oh, no! You are probably thinking that discipline is the last word you want to hear in association with developing healthier habits, but God shows us how much we can gain if we only persevere.

> No discipline seems pleasant at the time, but painful. Later on, however, it produces a harvest of righteousness and peace for those who have been trained by it.
> ### *Hebrews 12:11*

> And the God of all grace, who called you to his eternal glory in Christ, after you have suffered a little while, will himself restore you and make you strong, firm, and steadfast.
> ### *1 Peter 5:10*

Changing our daily habits can be painful, and it will take discipline. As you learn more this week about how your daily habits affect all aspects of your health, I pray that you will discover how making a few changes can have a multitude of positive results as you seek a healthier lifestyle.

DAY 1—PHYSICAL

Therefore, since we are surrounded by such a great cloud of witnesses, let us throw off everything that hinders and the sin that so easily entangles. And let us run with perseverance the race marked out for us, fixing our eyes on Jesus, the pioneer and perfecter of faith.

Hebrews 12:1–2a

We talk a great deal about our physical health during the first six weeks of our Bible study. We've discussed the importance of regular exercise and healthy eating to enable us to reach our goal of physical wellness, and we've emphasized avoiding risky health behaviors as we work to achieve our quest for a healthy temple to house the Holy Spirit within us.

The Apostle Paul used the metaphor of running or completing the race to describe his purpose in serving Jesus. Paul recognized that this "race" would be a tough one. Taking care of our body physically is a challenge. There are so many variables: making healthy choices about what we eat, exercising regularly, getting adequate rest, avoiding too much sun, being careful of chemical exposure and pollution, coping appropriately with stress, getting adequate treatment when we're sick, etc. The list goes on and on, but keep in mind that our goal is to reach our fullest potential in service to our Lord.

Please read 1 Corinthians 9:24–27

What are some roadblocks you experience as you run this "race" toward achieving a healthier lifestyle?

_____

_____

_____

_____

_____

The good news is that our body doesn't rule us—we are in charge of the decisions we make! God will provide us with the strength and courage to make the right choices that lead us to a healthier lifestyle.

Our Prayer: Father, the race is hard. It's a challenge to keep going. I pray You will be with me and each member of our group as we strive toward the challenge of a healthy temple for the Holy Spirit.

DAY 2—INTELLECTUAL/ MENTAL

Do not conform to the pattern of this world, but be transformed by the renewing of your mind. Then you will be able to test and approve what God's will is—his good, pleasing, and perfect will.

Romans 12:2

The human brain weighs about three pounds and is made primarily of water and fat. Our brain is of vital importance since it controls everything about our bodies. Below are some ways we can keep our brains healthy.

- Exercise (especially aerobic exercise) benefits our brains, and it's never too late to start.
- Stay socially and intellectually active. Read, learn new things, play games that stimulate the brain, and maintain healthy relationships with others.
- Eat a healthy diet. Research has shown that certain foods are particularly good for brain health—leafy greens, beets, tomatoes,

avocados, nuts (especially walnuts), blueberries, fish, red grapes, olive oil, coffee, and dark chocolate (nuts, avocados, olive oil, and chocolate should be eaten in small quantities due to the high fat content). Most of these are the same foods that are good for our heart!

- Get enough (good) sleep.
- Keep your heart healthy (e.g., control blood pressure, LDL cholesterol, diabetes). While medication can help control these issues, making positive diet changes is highly effective for maintaining a healthy heart.

Prayerfully review this list again. What is one thing you can select from this list to act on as you work toward a healthier you?

_____

_____

_____

_____

_____

Our Prayer: Father, thank You for being with us on this journey. Change is hard! We get used to our old habits and choosing new and challenging lifestyle changes is scary. I'm worried that I might fail. But You are the God of second chances. You know we aren't perfect, yet You love us anyway. Please give us the strength to persevere and to try again when we mess up.

DAY 3—EMOTIONAL AND SOCIAL

Please read John 11:1–36. Jesus was deeply moved by Mary and Martha's sorrow as well as the death of his friend Lazarus, and *"Jesus wept."* Jesus was not afraid to express his emotions.

Jesus maintained close relationships with his disciples. He even called them friends.

> "My command is this: Love each other as I have loved you. Greater love has no one than this: to lay down one's life for one's friends. You are my friends if you do what I command. I no longer call you servants, because a servant does not know his master's business. Instead I have called you friends, for everything that I learned from my Father I have made known to you."
>
> ### *John 15:12–15*

Relationships are important to our social and emotional health. God did not mean for us to be alone or to isolate ourselves. He gifted us with the joy of family, friendships, marriage, and our fellowship with our church family so that we could fulfill His command to "**love one another as I have loved you**" (**John 13:34**).

1 Samuel describes the strong friendship between David and Jonathan. Jonathan loved his friend and protected David at the risk of his own life when his father, Saul, was trying to kill David.

So Jonathan made a covenant with the house of David, saying, "May the Lord call David's enemies to account." And Jonathan had David reaffirm his oath out of love for him, because he loved him as he loved himself.

1 Samuel 20:16–17

Please list some ways that your friends show love to you and that you show love to your friends.

_____

_____

_____

_____

_____

Our Prayer: Thank You for the gift of love, Father. Thank You for family and friends. I'm grateful for the supportive group of friends that You have surrounded me with during this Bible study. I pray for each member of our group, that You will continue to guide us on our journey toward wellness.

DAY 4—VOCATIONAL

In this context, we're using the word "vocation" to encompass occupation, purpose in life, and service to others. Wow! That's a lot!

Some of us are retired. Many are employed, full- or part-time. Each of us is likely juggling numerous family responsibilities. But we all have a purpose in life. If you're like me, you may still be struggling to figure out what that is.

After his conversion, The Apostle Paul seemed to have no problem knowing his purpose.

"And now, compelled by the Spirit, I am going to Jerusalem, not knowing what will happen to me there. I only know that in every city the Holy spirit warns me that prison and hardships are facing me. However, I consider my life worth nothing to me; my only aim is to finish the race and complete the task the Lord Jesus has given me—the task of testifying to the good news of God's grace."
Acts 20:22–24

We are expected to work for the Lord. Please read James 2:14–26. We're not only called to serve our Lord through our words and witness but also through our actions. Faith is of vital importance, but by itself, faith is not enough. James tells us we must act on that faith.

As the body without the spirit is dead, so faith without deeds is dead.

James 2:26

But what does this mean? What do you think James is telling us to do?

_____

_____

_____

_____

Sometimes we are overwhelmed by the number of needs we see—situations may be calling for our assistance, yet our lives are so busy we can't find the time to get involved to help others. If you had the opportunity, what are some things you feel called to do to help others but haven't been able to get started on?

_____

_____

_____

_____

Our Prayer: Father, we are getting into some hard questions. Please be with us as we do some soul searching and reflect upon our purpose and how we can best serve You.

DAY 5—SPIRITUAL

Seek first his kingdom and his righteousness, and all these
things will be given to you as well.
Matthew 6:33

Spirituality involves a relationship; it is an understanding of the gift of
grace received from a being that transcends us. The giver determines the
relationship, but the recipient is expected to recognize the gift and be
actively engaged in a relationship with the giver.[14]

For Christians, God is this transcendent Being (Father, Son, and
Holy Spirit) and we are, of course, greatly nurtured by this relationship.
God is our Creator, the giver of life, and Jesus is our gift of grace, our
source of eternal life.

Please read John 4:27–38.

Again, food is used as a metaphor in this scripture, a symbol for
something greater. Jesus tells the disciples that He has "**food to eat that
they know nothing about**." We are blessed to have the Bible, the record-
ing of the teachings and actions of our Lord. The disciples were living in
that moment; they didn't have what we now call the New Testament. We
have the benefit of knowing "the rest of the story."[15]

When Jesus speaks of spiritual food and "**living water**" (**John 4:10–13**), what does He mean? Where do you get your spiritual food? How can we strengthen our spiritual health? How can we apply what we've learned thus far to our spiritual growth?

_____

_____

_____

_____

_____

Please read John 6:35–51.

Our Prayer: Father, thank You for the gift of Your Son. Jesus our Savior is our bread of life and through Him we have eternal life. We are so blessed. Please continue to guide us on our journey to honor our Savior and Holy Spirit with a healthy temple in which He may dwell.

REFLECTIONS ON WEEK SEVEN: THE DIMENSIONS OF HEALTH

Then the king ordered Ashpenaz, chief of his court officials, to bring into the king's service some of the Israelites from the royal family and the nobility—young men without any physical defect, handsome, showing aptitude for every kind of learning, well informed, quick to understand, and qualified to serve in the king's palace.

Daniel 1:3–4a

Reflect on how Daniel and his friends illustrate the dimensions of health (physical, intellectual/mental, emotional, social, vocational, and spiritual health).

_____

_____

_____

_____

_____

What about you? Obviously, none of us is perfect (and won't be on this Earth), but we want to be operating at our fullest potential to better serve God. Briefly analyze how you are doing in each area. (And remember, this is a journey toward wellness, and we are still in the early stages. Don't beat yourself up.)

_____

_____

_____

_____

_____

If you wish, take a few moments to reflect on what you feel may be your purpose in life.

_____

_____

_____

_____

_____

WEEK EIGHT:

We are Sanctified

Goals for Week Eight

1. Discover the meaning of sanctification.
2. Discuss the relationship between sanctification and holiness.
3. Reaffirm God's gift of saving grace through Jesus Christ.
4. Reflect on what this means for us.

WE ARE CHOSEN AND LOVED BY GOD

In the first week of our Bible study, we discussed how our body is a temple for the Holy Spirit. You will also recall that when Jesus knew He was going to be separated from the disciples by His earthly death, He sent the Holy Spirit as a Comforter and Counselor to His disciples (and to us). Early in His ministry, Jesus spoke to Nicodemus of the Spirit.

> "Very truly I tell you, no one can enter the kingdom of God unless they are born of water and the Spirit. Flesh gives birth to flesh, but the Spirit gives birth to spirit. You should not be surprised at my saying, 'You must be born again.' The wind blows whenever it pleases. You hear its sound but you cannot tell where it comes from or where it is going. So it is with everyone born of the Spirit."
>
> *John 3:5–8*

Nicodemus, as we know, struggled with this concept of being "born again." He asked, "Can I enter again into my mother's womb?" As Christians, we know that "being born again" is becoming a new creation in the Body of Christ. Jesus gave himself in atonement for our sins, granting us the gift of eternal life with Him. Our recognition of this is necessary for our salvation. When we accept that Jesus is our Savior, we are "filled" with the Holy Spirit—and we are a new creation in Christ.

For the one whom God has sent speaks the words of God, for God gives the Spirit without limit. The Father loves the Son and has placed everything in his hands.
John 3:34–35

God loves us! He loves us so much that He sacrificed His Son for us. Jesus took our sins upon himself so that we could live. Jesus loved us so much that He accepted the punishment we deserve.

But he was pierced for our transgressions, he was crushed for our iniquities; the punishment that brought us peace was on him and by his wounds we are healed.
Isaiah 53:5

In Paul's letter to the Ephesians, he wrote:

You were taught in regard to your former way of life, to put off your old self, which is being corrupted by its deceitful desires, to be made new in the attitude of your minds; and to put on the new self, created to be like God in true righteousness and holiness.
Ephesians 4:22–24

Last week, our closing scripture reminded us that we are "God's chosen people, a Holy nation." This week we will talk about what that means. For now, isn't it awesome and amazing to recognize that we are chosen and loved by God?

It is amazing grace!

DAY 1

But we ought always to thank God for you, brothers and sisters loved by the Lord, because God chose you as firstfruits to be saved through the sanctifying work of the Spirit and through belief in the truth. He called you to this through our gospel, that you might share in the glory of our Lord Jesus Christ. So then, brothers and sisters, stand firm and hold fast to the teachings we passed on to you, whether by word of mouth or by letter. May our Lord Jesus Christ himself and God our Father, who loved us and by his grace gave us eternal encouragement and good hope, encourage your hearts and strengthen you in every good deed and word.

2 Thessalonians 2:13–16

Paul wrote this letter to the church at Thessalonica early in his ministry. He praised them for their faith and provided instruction and encouragement.

Please list three or four important messages from the scripture above that apply to our lives today.

_____

_____

_____

_____

_____

It is God's will that you should be sanctified: that you should avoid sexual immorality; that each of you should learn to control your own body in a way that is holy and honorable, not in passionate lust like the pagans, who do not know God; and that in this matter no one should wrong or take advantage of a brother or sister. The Lord will punish all those who commit such sins, as we told you and warned you before. For God did not call us to be impure, but to live a holy life. Therefore, anyone who rejects this instruction does not reject a human being, but God, the very God who gives you his Holy Spirit.

1 Thessalonians 4:3–8

Please read the next to last sentence of that scripture again.

For God did not call us to be impure, but to live a holy life.

Wow! We knew that—didn't we? But when I'm reminded of this, it gives me a quivery feeling in my stomach. What about you? To know God is calling us to live holy lives and that He will guide us on that that journey—_and_ He will give us the ability to control our decisions and behavior—is awesome!

DAY 2

Therefore, with minds that are alert and fully sober, set your hope on the grace to be brought to you when Jesus Christ is revealed at his coming. As obedient children, do not conform to the evil desires you had when you lived in ignorance. But just as he who called you is holy, so be holy in all you do; for it is written: "Be holy, because I am holy."

1 Peter 1:13–16

So, what does it mean to be sanctified?

When something is sanctified, the person or object is set apart for the use of its designer.[16] In the Christian context, objects or people are sanctified or holy when they are set apart for God's purposes.[17] Christ is both the Sanctifier and the model of sanctification. Through God's plan of sanctifying grace, He sent Jesus to be the means of our sanctification. We are made Holy through the blood and sacrifice of Jesus Christ.

In Greek, the word for holiness is *hagiasmos*. It means to reflect what God is, to be clean and pure. *Sanctified*, in Greek, is also referred to as *hagiasmos*. The words are often used interchangeably in the New Testament.[18]

People of God are called to holiness and are sanctified through the sacrifice of Jesus. This is part of God's purpose for us since He is our designer. We are set apart for service to our Lord.

Reflect on what being set apart for God's purpose means to you—to be clean, pure, and holy for God's service and purpose. If you don't have enough room here, there is space on this week's reflection page.

_____

_____

_____

_____

_____

Our Prayer: Father, now that we've learned what sanctified means, it's kind of scary! To know that we are set apart for Your purpose, to be Holy and pure for You is really scary. Help each of us to trust You, to have faith, to believe in Your promise that You will be with us every step of our journey.

DAY 3

How do we become sanctified?

Please read John 17 (the entire chapter).

Jesus prayed for His disciples and prayed for us when he said:

> "My prayer is not for them alone. I pray also for those who will believe in me through their message, that all of them may be one, Father, just as you are in me and I am in you. May they also be in us so that the world may believe that you have sent me."
>
> **_John 17:20–22_**

The Apostle Paul, recognized as the greatest missionary for Jesus, describes his calling to serve his Lord and his own journey to sanctification. On the road to Damascus, Jesus said to Paul:

> "I am Jesus, whom you are persecuting," the Lord replied. "Now get up and stand on your feet. I have appeared to you to appoint you as a servant and as a witness of what you have seen and will see of me. I will rescue you from your own people

and from the Gentiles. I am sending you to them to open their eyes and turn them from darkness to light, and from the power of Satan to God, so that they may receive forgiveness of sins and a place among those who are sanctified by faith in me."
Acts 26:15–18

Please read Romans 15:14–16.

Paul took his duty seriously. He worked vigorously, often in extreme danger, to share the Gospel of Jesus so that believers could receive sanctification. We have received the benefits of Paul's instruction to the Gentiles. Just like the believers in the time of Paul and the other apostles, we are chosen to be sanctified through the loving sacrifice of Jesus our Lord and Savior.

Our Prayer: Father, how wonderful to know that You have chosen me, that You have set me apart for Your purpose. I pray that You will show us our path and the purpose for which You have chosen us and that You will guide us on our journey toward wellness so that we may be able to serve You with our very best.

DAY 4

Make every effort to live in peace with everyone and to be
holy; without holiness no one will see the Lord.
Hebrews 12:14

Please read Romans 6:19–23.

We are reminded that, as those set apart for the work of God (sanctified), we are holy. Furthermore, we are to be holy in all that we do—not
just on Sunday when in the house of the Lord but in "everyday life."
What are some tasks we can do (or are doing) that show we are set apart
for the purpose of God? Please list a few of your ideas either in a separate
journal or on this week's reflection page.

Fasting was a practice used both by the Israelites in their early history
and by Christians and Jews in New Testament times. Fasting helps people
practice self-control and discipline and promotes spiritual growth. Jesus
fasted for forty days and nights in preparation for the beginning of His
ministry (Matthew 4:1–4).[19] Fasting can include a total abstention from
food or partial limitations in diet. Vegetarians and vegans practice a type
of fasting (as did Daniel). Many Christians will limit certain types of
food during Lent as part of a discipline and self-denial plan to strengthen

their faith and mentally prepare for the celebration of Holy Week and the Resurrection. Some diets include partial fasting as a cleansing phase. Have you ever fasted? How did it make you feel? Can you reflect on the practice of fasting as a way to help us purify ourselves for service to the Lord? (Remember, we are set apart for God's purpose.) Can you consider fasting as a practice to help you become more holy rather than to help you lose weight?

_____

_____

_____

_____

_____

Our Prayer: Father, we are seeking to become pure and holy because we know we are set apart for Your purpose. It's scary, and we need Your help and guidance on this journey.

DAY 5

It is because of him (God) that you are in Christ Jesus, who has
become for us wisdom from God—that is, our righteousness,
holiness, and redemption.
1 Corinthians 1:30

Oswald Chambers writes that the secret of living a holy life is allowing
the "perfect qualities of Jesus to exhibit themselves in ... human flesh."
These qualities include patience, love, holiness, faith, purity, and godli-
ness. According to Chambers, in order to be sanctified, we must give ourselves completely to God. He says, "Sanctification is not something Jesus
puts in me it is *Himself* in me." To further clarify how the process works,
Chambers states, "Sanctification is not drawing from Jesus the power to
be holy—it is drawing from Jesus the very holiness that was exhibited in
Him, and that He now exhibits in me."[20]

This requires a total submission of our will to Jesus Christ so that
we are filled with the Holy Spirit, thus His very holiness is imparted
to us.

Paul writes to the Colossians about how this process works in his
service to the church:

I have become its servant by the commission God gave me to present to you the word of God in its fullness—the mystery that has been kept hidden for ages and generations, but is now disclosed to the Lord's people. To them God has chosen to make known among the Gentiles the glorious riches of this mystery, which is Christ in you, the hope of glory.

Colossians 1:25–27

We are chosen! God chose us, and Jesus is the instrument by which we are sanctified. Thanks be to God! However, we must not forget that with these gifts of salvation and sanctification comes the responsibility of service to our Lord.

May God himself, the God of peace, sanctify you through and through. May your whole spirit, soul and body be kept blameless at the coming of our Lord Jesus Christ. The one who calls you is faithful, and he will do it.

1 Thessalonians 5:23–24

REFLECTIONS ON WEEK EIGHT: WE ARE SANCTIFIED

But you are a chosen people, a royal priesthood, a holy nation, God's special possession, that you may declare the praises of him who called you out of darkness into his wonderful light.

1 Peter 2:9

Remember, we are chosen!

May God himself, the God of peace, sanctify you through and through. May your whole spirit, soul and body be kept blameless at the coming of our Lord Jesus Christ. The one who calls you is faithful, and he will do it.

1 Thessalonians 5:23

We read the above verse during our last daily reading this week, but I feel like it is powerful enough to read again before we reflect on God's plan for us.

Please read Romans 8:31–39.

We are reminded that through the love of God and the sacrifice of Jesus, we are sanctified. Paul also tells us that nothing can separate us from the love of God. How should we respond to this awesome gift of love? How does knowing that you are sanctified—"set apart" for the Lord's work—make you feel?

_____

_____

_____

_____

_____

Are you confused about what God has "set you apart" for? If so, you're not alone. Even Mother Teresa, as dedicated to God and service as she was, had times when she struggled with faith and purpose. I pray that you continue to seek God's presence and guidance during times of discouragement and doubt. Sanctification is a lifelong journey:

> "The growth of trees and plants takes place so slowly that it is not easily seen. Daily we notice little change. But, in the course of time, we see that a great change has taken place. So it is with grace. Sanctification is a progressive, lifelong work."
> John Owen

WEEK NINE:

Be a Light

Goals for Week Nine

1. Recognize that we are part of God's plan to spread the Gospel of Jesus—we are a light for Jesus!
2. Acknowledge that serving God and being a light for Jesus brings light to a dark world.
3. Reflect on our gifts and how we can use them in service to our Lord.
4. Continue with our journey toward wellness so that we are "fit for service" to our Lord.
5. Continue to encourage, love, and support our sisters and brothers in Christ on our ongoing journey to honor God with our bodies so that we may serve Him to our fullest potential.

BE FIT FOR SERVICE

What does being a light or being fit for service mean?
David writes in Psalm 37:5–6:

Commit your way to the Lord; trust in him and he will do this:
He will make your righteous reward shine like the dawn, your
vindication like the noonday sun.

David is sharing God's lifetime plan for us—*trust him*. Trust God.
Believe in His love as demonstrated through the gift of Jesus our Savior.
Earlier in our Bible study, we read 2 Corinthians 5:17.

Therefore, if anyone is in Christ, the new creation has come:
The old has gone, the new is here!

The next verses in Chapter 5 remind us what we are to do with our
"new" selves.

All this is from God, who reconciled us to himself through
Christ and gave us the ministry of reconciliation: that God

was reconciling the world to himself in Christ, not counting people's sins against them. And he has committed to us the message of reconciliation. We are therefore Christ's ambassadors, as though God were making his appeal through us. We implore you on Christ's behalf: Be reconciled to God.

2 Corinthians 5:18–20

Paul reminds us in his letter to Titus what Christ's gift of salvation requires of us in response.

Remind the people to be subject to rulers and authorities, to be obedient, to be ready to do whatever is good, to slander no one, to be peaceable and considerate, and always to be gentle toward everyone. At one time we too were foolish, disobedient, deceived and enslaved by all kinds of passions and pleasures. We lived in malice and envy, being hated and hating one another. But when the kindness and love of God our Savior appeared, he saved us, not because of the righteous things we had done, but because of his mercy. He saved us through the washing of rebirth and renewal by the Holy Spirit, whom he poured out on us generously through Jesus Christ our Savior, so that, having been justified by his grace, we might become heirs having the hope of eternal life.

Titus 3:1–7

We are called to be ambassadors for Christ, to be obedient to our Lord, to be peaceable, considerate, kind, compassionate, and gentle—to do whatever is good—and to let our light shine in service to Jesus.

A LIGHT OF SERVICE

In January of 2000, my mother passed away suddenly. It's never easy to say goodbye to a loved one. Those of you who have experienced that pain understand the hurt and loss. As we planned her funeral, my family allowed me the privilege of selecting songs for my mother's service. One of the ones I chose was "Be a Light." This is a rollicking, joyous tune—not the typical funeral song. The message of the song is that we should be a light for Jesus always, every single day. My mother lived this command. She exemplified Christian service in all things and is my hero.

> For we are God's handiwork, created in Christ Jesus to do good works, which God prepared in advance for us to do.
> ***Ephesians 2:10***

In the first weeks of our time together in this Bible study, we were reminded of how much God loves us—so much that He sent His only Son to take our sin upon himself and sacrifice himself for us. Paul writes to the Ephesians:

> I pray that out of his glorious riches he may strengthen you with power through his Spirit in your inner being, so that Christ may dwell in your hearts through faith. And I pray that you, being rooted and established in love, may have power, together with all the Lord's holy people, to grasp how wide and long and high and deep is the love of Christ, and to know this

love that surpasses knowledge—that you may be filled to the
measure of all the fullness of God.
Ephesians 3:16–19

Our response is to love one another as God has loved us—thus to
live a life in praise of God, honoring Him through our work of witness
and service.

As we continue to grow in our faith and become more like Christ,
we will become more devoted to a life of service. Jesus told His disciples:

"For even the Son of Man did not come to be served, but to
serve, and to give his life as a ransom for many."
Mark 10:45

Jesus is not calling us to sacrifice our lives in the same way that he
did. There are many ways that we can give of ourselves and place the
needs of others before our own. In service to our Lord, we "die" in the
sense that we become less self-centered and are able to love others in the
manner Jesus has demonstrated. Jesus said:

"Whoever serves me must follow me; and where I am,
my servant also will be. My Father will honor the one who
serves me."
John 12:26

This week, we discuss the gifts we were given by God and how we can
use those gifts in service to God's children.

DAY 1

The people walking in darkness have seen a great light; on those living in the land of deep darkness a light has dawned.

Isaiah 9:2

When Jesus spoke again to the people, he said, "I am the light of the world. Whoever follows me will never walk in darkness, but will have the light of life."

John 8:12

Please read John 1:1–9.

Jesus is the "**true light that gives help to everyone**." That includes us! And don't forget, Jesus sent us the Holy Spirit as our Counselor and Guide. As you might remember from our first week, our body is the temple that provides the dwelling place for the Holy Spirit, and our quest is to make that temple as healthy as possible for the Holy Spirit.

How wonderful that the Holy Spirit is always with us! Paul writes in Romans:

In the same way, the Spirit helps us in our weakness. We do not know what we ought to pray for, but the Spirit himself intercedes for us through wordless groans. And he who searches our hearts knows the mind of the Spirit, because the Spirit intercedes for God's people in accordance to the will of God. And we know that in all things God works for the good of those who love him, who have been called according to his purpose.

Romans 8:26–28

This week, I'm going to have you ask yourself some hard questions. Remember, the Holy Spirit is with you. I'm praying for you.

Our Prayer: Father, we know that Jesus is the Light of the world and that You sent Him as a gift of love to us. I know You love us so much, Father, but sometimes I forget You love me! You have led us through this Bible study, and we've examined some things that have been hard to accept. Now I'm going to need to search even deeper. Please continue to be with me and each member of our group as we work through this final week of study. Please stay with us even after we finish because we want to maintain our journey toward wellness so that the Holy Spirit will always have a healthy temple in which to dwell.

DAY 2

"No one lights a lamp and hides it in a clay jar or puts it under a bed. Instead, they put it on a stand, so that those who come in can see the light."

Luke 8:16

That verse from Luke is Jesus speaking to his disciples. In the following verse from Paul's letter to the Corinthians, Paul is spreading the Gospel of Jesus.

For what we preach is not ourselves, but Jesus Christ as Lord, and ourselves as your servants for Jesus' sake. For God, who said, "Let light shine out of darkness," made his light shine in our hearts to give us the light of the knowledge of God's glory displayed in the face of Christ.

2 Corinthians 4:5–6

Please also read John 3:16–21.

The message is clear, in these scriptures and throughout the New Testament: Jesus is the Light! And, as His children, His followers, and His witness to the world, we are also called to be a light for others.

Remember our beginning goal for our study? We are on a journey toward wellness so that we can honor God with our bodies. The Holy Spirit, sent by Jesus, dwells within us in our temple—our body. We want that temple to be as healthy as possible so that we may serve our Lord. We want to be the brightest light for Jesus as we can be.

The unfolding of your words gives light; it gives understanding to the simple.

Psalm 119:130

Our Prayer: Father, sometimes we struggle to understand Your purpose for us. I pray You will guide each of us to seek light through Your words as we continue our journey to a closer relationship with You.

DAY 3

For in you is the fountain of life; in your light we see light.
Psalm 36:9

But you are a chosen people, a royal priesthood, a holy nation, God's special possession, that you may declare the praises of him who called you out of darkness into his wonderful light.
1 Peter 2:9

As a prisoner for the Lord, then, I urge you to live a life worthy of the calling you have received. Be completely humble and gentle, be patient, bearing with one another in love. Make every effort to keep the unity of the Spirit through the bond of peace.
Ephesians 4:1–3

Please read 2 Corinthians 9:6–15.

We are called to serve our Lord. I know we don't like to admit we have gifts (talents) that God has given us. But we do! God has made each of us unique. Remember, we are **"fearfully and wonderfully made."** So, please put away your pride and list a few things that you are good at—talents or gifts that God has given you—that you can use in service to others.

_____

_____

_____

_____

_____

Our Prayer: Father, we are taught to be humble, so it's hard to describe our talents. It seems like bragging, but the Bible tells us to use our gifts in service to You, thus we need to examine those blessings so that we can discover where we can best serve You. Please help!

The Lord is my light and my salvation—whom shall I fear? The Lord is the stronghold of my life—of whom shall I be afraid?
Psalm 27:1

DAY 4

As for you, brothers and sisters, never tire of doing what is good.
2 Thessalonians 3:18

There are different kinds of gifts, but the same Spirit distributes them. There are different kinds of service, but the same Lord. There are different kinds of working, but in all of them and in everyone it is the same God at work ... All of these are the work of one and the same Spirit, and he distributes them to each one, just as he determines.
1 Corinthians 12:4–6, 11

Let us not become weary in doing good, for at the proper time we will reap a harvest if we do not give up. Therefore, as we have opportunity, let us do good to all people, especially to those who belong to the family of believers.
Galatians 6:9–10

In the previous daily reading, I asked you to list some of the gifts, talents, and blessings that God has given you. If you doubt that you have gifts, please read 1 Corinthians 12. According to God's Word, we all have gifts! (If you didn't list your gifts yet, please go back and do so). Today, please prayerfully consider where there are needs. These needs may be in your family, neighborhood, church, place of work, hospitals or nursing homes, an agency, charitable organizations, etc. List a few people or places you know need help.

_____

_____

_____

_____

_____

Our Prayer: Father, I pray for Your guidance as we think about those in need and how we can use the gifts You have given us to help. Please guide us as we look out into the world and seek ways to serve You.

Thy Word is a Lamp for my feet and a light for my path.
Psalm 119:105

DAY 5

Through Jesus, therefore, let us continually offer to God a sacrifice of praise—the fruit of lips that openly profess his name. And do not forget to do good and to share with others, for with such sacrifices God is pleased.
Hebrews 13:15–16

And this is my prayer that your love may abound more and more in knowledge and depth of insight, so that you may be able to discern what is best and may be pure and blameless for the day of Christ, filled with the fruit of righteousness that comes through Jesus Christ—to the glory and praise of God.
Philippians 1:9–11

Please read Isaiah 49:1–6.

God has a plan for us to serve Him. He sent His Son to us as the Light of the world, and we are called to actively spread that light through worship, witness, and service.

Jesus said, "You are the light of the world. A town built on a hill cannot be hidden. Neither do people light a lamp and put it under a bowl. Instead they put it on its stand, and it gives light to everyone in the house. In the same way, let your light shine before others, that they may see your good deeds and glorify your Father in heaven."

Matthew 5:14–16

Jesus reminds us to "let our light shine." When we are good to others, God is glorified. How awesome is that? By showing kindness to our family, friends, coworkers, and neighbors, we bring glory to God and fulfill the teachings of Jesus. But sometimes it's hard to know who we are called to help. For instance, who is our neighbor? Please read Luke 10:25–37.

After reading that, who is your neighbor?

_____

_____

_____

_____

_____

Jesus said:

"Whoever serves me must follow me; and where I am, my servant also will be. My Father will honor the one who serves me."

John 12:26

What is God calling you to do to spread the Light of Jesus to others? Please respond on this week's reflection page.

REFLECTIONS ON WEEK NINE: BE A LIGHT FOR JESUS

This is the message we have heard from him and declare to you: God is light; in him there is not darkness at all. If we claim to have fellowship with him and yet walk in the darkness, we lie and do not live out the truth. But if we walk in the light, as he is in the light, we have fellowship with one another, and the blood of Jesus, his Son, purifies us from all sin.

1 John 1:5–7

After prayerful consideration, what do you feel God is calling you to do in service to Him? How can you use your gifts to be a Light for Jesus?

_____

_____

_____

_____

Being a servant in God's kingdom is our calling, but we are not expected to complete every task ourselves. How can you serve as a role model and mentor for others in your church and community?

_____

_____

_____

_____

_____

SAYING GOODBYE—AND
WHAT TO DO NOW

We've been together nine weeks—working, studying, delving into God's word, learning about wellness, reflecting on our journey, and examining how we can change our lifestyle to help us find the pathway to better health. We've been seeking balance and harmony.

Please think about the orchestra as I compared it to our relationship with Christ in the first week of this Bible study. God, the composer of all Creation, authored an awesome musical score (the Earth and all who inhabit it). The orchestra (us) works together in balance and harmony, practicing faithfully to achieve their best performance (we learn the pathway to all aspects of wellness and service). The conductor (Jesus) mentors, guides, and directs the entire process of our spiritual, physical, mental, intellectual, emotional, and vocational growth. The subsequent performance brings excitement, joy, and appreciation to all who are blessed to hear it (our life of service to Christ brings joy to us and others.)

Simon Peter Iredale uses dancers to illustrate this point. We are astonished by the amazing skill and beauty of dancers. Their extraordinary artistry and ability make their performance seem effortless, yet we only see this beautiful "fruit" because of thousands of hours of practice, physical pain, injuries, and great dedication and sacrifice.[21]

Iredale compares this performance to the Christian life. To the observer, the Christian journey may seem effortless and easy, but this relationship with Christ doesn't come without a lifetime of commitment and work. In this Christian journey, we are not simply practicing Christian actions; through constant study, practice, and discipline, we are becoming the person Christ has called us to be. The Christian disciple is, like the dancer, living a lifetime of discipline and sacrifice to follow Christ.

During this Bible study, we have focused on developing the knowledge and tools we need to guide our body toward wellness so that our temple for the Holy Spirit can be housed in a vessel (our body) that is healthy and happy. This will take continued study of the Bible and an ongoing effort to maintain our spiritual relationship. Our journey will require practice (developing healthy habits) and discipline (changing unhealthy lifestyle habits into good ones).

We've come to the end of our nine-week journey, but I pray you will continue on your journey toward wellness. Thank you for being part of our Bible study. May God bless you!

I'm praying for you!

Please feel free to contact me by email with questions. You can also find me on social media at the sites listed below.

Email: katherinepasour@gmail.com
Website and blog: www.katherinepasour.com
Facebook: Sheltered by an Angel's Wings, Katherine Pasour Author
Twitter: @KatherinePasour
Instagram: KatherinePasourAuthor

ABOUT THE AUTHOR

Katherine Pasour is an author, teacher, and speaker with a passion for both her own wellness and the wellness of others. She has taught wellness classes for people of all ages, from young adult to retirement and beyond.

Healthful living is not just about what we eat or how active we are, although those two aspects of health are very important. Achieving good health involves recognizing the many dimensions of health: physical, mental, spiritual, emotional, social, and vocational. These aspects intertwine, each one affecting the others. When all facets of health are balanced and viewed as important, we can strive for better health. Katherine's vocation—her call to serve—focuses on positively influencing others to make healthy lifestyle choices.

Katherine has degrees in health and physical education, religion, and a PhD in education. Her teaching career spans more than four decades during which she taught physical education to elementary children, taught wellness to young adults, and prepared students to be teachers. Katherine has led numerous Bible studies in her church and community. She recently retired as a professor and administrator at Lenoir-Rhyne University in Hickory, North Carolina. The "teaching bug" hasn't let go, and Katherine continues to teach part-time at the university while volunteering in numerous capacities in her church.

An outdoor girl at heart, Katherine enjoys her farm animals, gardening, and hiking. Although pulling weeds in her flowers isn't her favorite hobby, she finds the task a great stress reliever, especially in the spring, when the fruits of her labor display their glorious blossoms.

May God bless you on your journey to wellness.

Leader's Guide

ADDITIONAL RESOURCES FOR LEADERS

On the following pages, I have included suggestions for each week that the Bible study facilitator (leader) can use at their discretion.

Since there is significant emphasis on exercise and healthy nutrition, leaders should feel free to invite guest speakers in any area that could enhance the experience for the participants. Videos are also a possibility. I especially recommend the 2011 *Forks Over Knives* film (and additional resources from their website). It's an excellent resource for explaining how our diet impacts our overall health and how making changes can dramatically improve our health. More information on this film and other educational material is available at www.forksoverknives.com.

Exercising in groups or implementing the "buddy" system to encourage adding physical activity to our daily routine are effective strategies to increase and maintain physical activity. If you, as a leader, do not feel comfortable leading an exercise class, perhaps there is another volunteer who would. Exercising for an hour prior to the actual group meeting is one way to add physical activity in a supportive environment. Serving a healthy snack between exercise and the group meeting also encourages group interaction and provides an opportunity for sharing healthy recipes.

Other options for increasing physical activity include meeting at a park or track to walk if there is one available in your community. Many residential neighborhoods are also safe enough to allow walking on the streets or sidewalks. Other locations for walking could be a mall or any large store or building that will allow walkers. YMCAs, recreational facilities, and health clubs are good choices. Participants should have a partner or group to walk with, not only for the socialization and encouragement but also for safety.

Group members are encouraged to pray for each other. The group leader should lift up each participant in prayer daily. Other ways to assist the group on their journey to better health include encouraging emails, telephone calls, handwritten notes or cards exchanged in the group meeting, and the "good ole fashioned snail mail" version of encouragement (mailing cards).

WEEK ONE: INTRODUCTION SUGGESTIONS FOR THE LEADER

- Welcome and prayer.
- Read or share a devotional.
- Thank group for joining together on a "journey toward wellness."
- Have the group sign in (include their name, mailing address, telephone, and email).
- Check to see if some of the group members are willing to read aloud and, if desired, assign the following scriptures from Week One.
  - Read (or ask someone to read) 1 Corinthians 6:19–20; Discuss.
  - Read John 14:15–21 and remind participants that the Holy Spirit lives within us, God loves us, and Jesus loves us.
- Review keys points from Week One:
  - There are many dimensions of health (spiritual, physical, social, emotional, mental/intellectual, vocational) and all are interdependent.

- • Read Romans 12:4–8 and stress how the group is connected to, and encouraging of, each other. We'll pray for each other on our journey toward wellness.
- • It is vital to be in God's Word daily.
- If time allows, read Genesis 1:1–27 and Psalm 139:13–16. Discuss God's awesome and amazing Creation—which includes us!
- A Google search for "The Amazing Human Body" or "Awesome Facts about the Human Body" (or similar keywords) will reveal some interesting facts. If you wish to use this strategy, type or write some of these fascinating tidbits on cards or strips of paper and ask individuals to read them aloud to the group.
- Briefly review the format of this study. There is a short introduction, five daily readings, and a reflection page to complete each week. Participants will get much more out of the study if they complete these readings and responses in advance of the weekly meeting.
- Ask participants to write down something they expect or hope to learn during this Bible study on an index card.
- Ask for questions and/or prayer requests and close with prayer.

WEEK TWO: GOD LOVES YOU SUGGESTIONS FOR THE LEADER

- Welcome and prayer.
- Share a devotion focusing on God's great love for His people. You can ask for volunteers for future devotions and prayers.
- If you are using small groups, ask each group to share two or three blessings they have received this week within their group. If you are using the full group, share as time allows.
- Read or have participants read any of the following relevant scriptures focusing on wisdom and the Holy Spirit. Discuss the common theme in these scriptures and how this relates to our goal to achieve better health for our temple, our body which houses the Holy Spirit. One possible way to guide this discussion is to have small groups and assign one scripture to each group and have them lead the discussion on that particular scripture. Remind the group that God's word tells us that the Holy Spirit dwells within us and that Christ is the giver of wisdom. Thus, as Christians, we have the opportunity to gain wisdom. Although

there are many benefits to having the wisdom of Christ to guide our path, one important one is the knowledge of how to care for our bodies, to keep our temple healthy to honor God.

- Job 28:12–28
- 1 Corinthians 1:20–30
- 1 Corinthians 2:6–16
- 1 Corinthians 3:16–17

• Have a brief discussion about heredity (genetic makeup, traits, characteristics that we inherit) and environment (lifestyle choices like what we eat, whether we exercise or lead a sedentary lifestyle, whether we engage in risky behaviors such as tobacco use, our health habits, etc.) emphasizing that we cannot change who are parents are/were, but we can avoid risky health behaviors and begin new habits that will improve our health. Even if we inherit the tendency for a chronic disease, positive lifestyle choices can delay onset or prevent the development of the chronic disease.

• On the second day of the Bible study, participants were asked to list some risky behaviors or barriers keeping them from better health. Ask if anyone would be brave enough to share.

• Remind the group that this Bible study is a "safe place." What is discussed should remain confidential and members should feel comfortable sharing anything—past pain, current suffering, bad habits, plans to develop new habits, etc. It's important that we pray for each other throughout the study.

• We emphasized the importance of fruits and vegetables this week and preparing them in a healthy way while limiting any added sugar or fats. Ask members of the group if they were able to add fruits and vegetables prepared in a healthy way (fresh or frozen, not fried, avoiding rich sauces and butter, limiting salt, etc.). Remind participants that their goal is at least five servings of fruits and veggies each day.

- Have participants write on an index card what may be holding them back from making good health choices so that you can pray for them this week.
- Ask for comments, questions, and prayer requests.
- Close with prayer.

Tips to further the discussion above:

- Heredity—Our genetic makeup determines our skin, hair, eye color, etc., and sets up the template for our body type (height and bone structure). Our eating habits and activity level (environment) determine our weight. Sometimes certain chronic conditions tend to run in families (heart disease, hypertension, diabetes, cancer, etc.); however, our lifestyle choices, which are environmental (what we eat, how active we are, whether we smoke, etc.), have a large impact on our chances of developing or preventing these chronic diseases.
- Environment—From the day we are conceived, our environment begins to impact us. What the mother does when her child is in the womb greatly affects the health of the unborn child. From the day of birth, environment continues to have tremendous impact on our wellbeing. We may not be able to control where we live (e.g., exposure to smog or toxic chemicals), but we have a great deal of control over many things in our environment (e.g., wearing a seat belt, smoking, drug use, making healthy or unhealthy choices about what we eat, whether we are physically active).

WEEK THREE: LOVING OURSELVES AND OTHERS SUGGESTIONS FOR THE LEADER

- Welcome and prayer.
- Share a relevant devotional or have another member of the group do so.
- If you are brave enough, lead the group in singing "Jesus Loves Me."
- If group is not too large, and if time allows, ask participants how they did with adding more fruits and vegetables (prepared in a healthy way) to their diet this past week.
- Remind group that the emphasis for this week is "Loving Ourselves and Others."
- Read (or have someone read) any or all of the following scriptures:
  - John 13:34–35 (a review from last week, but important enough to share again!)
  - 1 John 4:7–10

- ▪ 1 John 4:13 through 1 John 5:5 (ask group to share some of their responses from Day 1 when they read this scripture and listed five important messages John is sharing with us).
- Ask group to share some challenges they experienced this week. Distribute index cards so that participants can write down a prayer request for you to pray about in the upcoming week.
- Read Luke 4:17–21. Discuss how Jesus came to free us from oppression and whatever might be holding us captive. Captivity can come in many forms and is often hard to recognize or identify. Take some time to talk in small groups. Participants may prefer to write on the same card rather than speak aloud about sensitive issues.
- Not everyone may wish to share about what may be holding them in captivity; however, it is likely that most everyone is experiencing some form of stress. Take a few minutes and allow the group to share some stressors in their lives. Small groups can brainstorm strategies to cope with stress or you may want to share some handouts focusing on dealing with stress. It's important for participants to realize that everyone experiences stress daily. Participants and leaders can find more information about stress in Appendix B.
- On Day 5 of this week, participants were asked to list up to five negative habits or lifestyle choices that might be unhealthy for them. Depending on the size of your group, allow small- or large-group discussion for anyone who wants to share some of their unhealthy behaviors. Some may wish to write these down on the same card as their challenges.
- For those who are willing to discuss a habit they want to change (eliminating an unhealthy behavior or adding a healthy behavior), the entire group can brainstorm strategies that can lead to positive change. In this supportive environment, participants will

recognize how meaningful group support can be in helping them to articulate goals and develop a plan to achieve healthy changes.

- For those who do not wish to share in front of the entire group, ask if they would like you to pray for them. If so, they can write down the behavior they wish to change so that you can pray for them in the upcoming week.
- Ask the group to pray for each other as they begin to take small steps toward making changes that will lead to a healthier lifestyle.
- Allow comments and questions. Remind group to keep all information shared confidential.
- Ask for prayer requests.

WEEK FOUR: JESUS WALKED SUGGESTIONS FOR THE LEADER

- Welcome and prayer
- Share a relevant devotional.
- Although the Bible doesn't tell us a lot about the health of Jesus and his disciples, the culture and habits of Jesus and the people who lived during his time were conducive to some healthy habits. Ask the group to share some behaviors that could have contributed to keeping Jesus healthy.
- Health-related physical fitness is important for every individual to achieve and maintain, no matter our age. Having good health-related fitness strengthens the heart and other muscles of the body; prevents heart disease, diabetes, and other chronic diseases; helps us maintain a healthy weight; reduces stress; helps prevent osteoporosis; stimulates our brain; and helps us live longer with a better quality of life.
- Review the five components of health-related physical fitness:

- **Cardiorespiratory endurance** is directly related to the health and strength of the heart muscle—the ability of the heart and lungs to work efficiently to allow an individual to perform sustained vigorous exercise over time. We strengthen our heart by working it harder than it is normally accustomed to (remind group to check with their healthcare provider before beginning an exercise program).
- **Muscular strength** is the maximum contractile ability of a muscle in a single contraction. We need muscular strength to lift heavy objects (e.g., carry groceries, move furniture, lift children and grandchildren).
- **Muscular endurance** is the ability of our muscles to perform sustained work over time. We need this type of fitness to perform everyday tasks (e.g., cleaning house, yardwork, climbing stairs) Again, we improve muscular strength and muscular endurance by working our muscles harder than what they are accustomed to. This can be done in the weight room, but an easier method is to use our own body for resistance (e.g., push-ups, squats, crunches, lunges). This meeting is a good opportunity for the leader or a guest to lead the participants through exercises that can be safely done at home during the week.
- **Flexibility** is range of motion—our ability to stretch. We need flexibility to accomplish our normal daily activities such as bending, reaching, and exercising. Good flexibility improves balance and helps prevent falls. For these reasons, daily stretching becomes more and more important as we age. Please have someone knowledgeable about safe stretching exercises demonstrate for the group.

- **Body composition** is the relationship between lean body mass and body fat. We improve body composition by eating a healthy diet and exercising regularly.
- Remind group that everyone needs to have good health-related fitness to maintain a good quality of life.
- Review the benefits of health-related fitness listed on Day 1 of this week's reading. Wow! Look what regular exercise can do for us! Remind the group that the Centers for Disease Control views regular exercise as a powerful method to positively improve our health and quality of life. And research shows that those who exercise regularly and maintain health-related fitness live a longer and healthier life.
- Ask the group: if regular exercise is such a "miracle cure" for so many things, why isn't everyone doing it?
- Discuss the benefits of walking. Remind group that working up to 150 or more minutes of walking (or other exercise) a week is their goal.
- Have group suggest strategies for adding more walking to their daily schedule. Can participants partner for walking or develop a plan for group exercise?
- Ask what has been holding them back from regular physical activity?
- Ask the group: what is one way you can increase your physical activity to work toward a healthier heart?
- Review FIT Principle
  - F—Frequency (how often you should exercise—three to five times per week)
  - I—Intensity (how hard you should work—enough to get the heart rate up and breathe faster)
  - T—Time (how long we should exercise—total of thirty to sixty minutes per day).

- T—Type (the type of exercise you choose will be affected by your goals and your preferences)
- V—Variety (we may become bored with the same routine; varying your routine can help prevent boredom and increase motivation)
- P—Progression (as your body becomes accustomed to exercise, you can add more time, intensity, or distance to continue to improve health-related fitness).
- Remind group that exercise time can be broken down into increments throughout the day.
- Ask for questions, comments, and prayer requests.
- Prayer.

WEEK FIVE: NEVER GIVE UP SUGGESTIONS FOR THE LEADER

- Welcome and prayer.
- Share a relevant devotion.
- In Week Two, participants were asked to select one action or one change that is a healthy lifestyle change (eliminating a negative health behavior or adding a positive one). It's check-up time! Ask the group (if they are willing) to share what the behavior is and what progress they are making. Praise and encourage them. Remind participants that you're praying for them.
- Ask several different participants to read the following scriptures aloud:
  - Galatians 1:10
  - Joshua 1:9
  - Ephesians 4:22–24
  - Ephesians 6:10–17
- Ask and allow responses and discussion for the following questions: What has tempted you this week? What doubts has Satan

put in your mind to convince you that you cannot succeed in developing healthy habits? Who or what is hindering you from your goal of making healthy changes? Who or what has encouraged you this week?

- God will give us the strength to resist the devil's temptations. God's word will also encourage us. Matthew 21:21–22 is an example you can read the group.

- Encourage the group to believe they can make healthy changes. Remind them to pray for each other.

- Ask the group whether they have been able to add physical activity this week. Allow time for sharing and discussion.

- On Day 5, participants were asked to pick a second lifestyle behavior to change. Allow each person (if they are willing) to share this new goal. If time allows, members of the group can offer suggestions that will assist in achieving this healthy behavior.

- On the Week Five's reflection page, participants were asked to select a scripture from the week that was especially encouraging to them. Ask if anyone is willing to share this scripture by reading to the group.

- Allow comments and questions. Ask for prayer requests.

- Ask participants to bring in several food labels each from a variety of foods to discuss in next week's group meeting.

- Close with prayer.

WEEK SIX: FEEDING THE TEMPLE SUGGESTIONS FOR THE LEADER

Some great sources to help you prepare for this week include:

- www.myplate.gov
- www.danielplan.com
- www.doctoroz.com
- www.fruitsandveggiesmorematters.org

There are many other great websites out there. A Google search for "Healthy Nutrition" will garner a lot of hits.

If you don't feel comfortable leading a session on healthy nutrition and the above sources and nutrition material in the appendices are not adequate, feel free to invite a nutritionist to be your speaker for this session.

- Welcome and prayer.
- A relevant devotion may be shared.

- The following scriptures offer insight on how our Biblical writers viewed food and demonstrate the prevalent metaphorical use of food in the Bible. A metaphor is figurative language or a phrase used to describe something that creates a vivid comparison.
  - Luke 8:1–15
  - Colossians 1:9b–10
  - Galatians 5:22–23
  - Psalm 63:4–5
  - Proverbs 12:14
  - Psalm 1:3
  - Jeremiah 17:7–8
  - Romans 7:4
- From these scriptures, we can see how powerful the use of food is in creating spiritual imagery.
- Review Appendix A to provide insight to participants about the six nutrients. We need foods from each of these groups daily. Our problem often arises when we eat too much of the unhealthy foods (refined sugar, saturated fat, fried foods, sweetened beverages, etc.) and not enough of the healthy foods (whole grains, fresh fruits and vegetables prepared in a healthy way, water, etc.).
- Discuss the importance of fiber (more information in Appendix D).
- Discuss the dangers of obesity (more information in Appendix C). Consider distributing a body mass index (BMI) chart. BMI is somewhat useful in helping people recognize whether they are overweight or obese; however, there are other more accurate measures. Any discussion of weight should be shared in a tactful way. Participants should be encouraged to speak with you privately or with a nutritionist or healthcare professional to discuss the dangers of obesity and develop weight management strategies.

- If time allows, discuss how to read food labels for important information—caloric and sodium content, portion size, nutrients, preservatives, chemical additives, etc.

- Sodium is an important mineral that works to regulate body fluids. Most Americans exceed healthy quantities of sodium in their daily diet. Fast foods, processed foods, snack foods, restaurant or deli food, and meat are particularly high in sodium. WebMD and MyPlate recommend no more than 2,300 mg of sodium per day. The American Heart Association encourages us to limit sodium to no more than 1,500 mg per day.

- On the reflection page for this week, participants were asked to write five positive habits they have in regard to eating habits. Ask if anyone in the group is willing to share aloud. This should be a time of affirmation and encouragement.

- Now for the hard part—ask the group if they are willing to share five things they need to change (in regard to nutrition) to become healthier. While this is not a time for affirmation (except from the standpoint of recognizing some of our dangerous habits), this *is* a time for encouragement as you ask participants if they are willing to pick one of these behaviors to focus on to make changes. Have the group (small or large) work together to develop strategies that each individual can use to make changes in their selected behavior.

- Ask for questions, comments, and prayer requests.
- Close with prayer.

WEEK SEVEN: THE DIMENSIONS OF HEALTH SUGGESTIONS FOR THE LEADER

- Welcome and prayer.
- Share a devotional if desired.
- Read (or ask someone to read) 1 Corinthians 9:24–27.
- God has bestowed upon us an amazing gift—our body! We are **"fearfully and wonderfully made."** What an awesome temple we have for the Holy Spirit. Paul reminds us that we must have a plan; we must be organized to achieve our goals. Our body is under our control, and with God's help, we *can* make changes that will lead to a healthier lifestyle.
- Remind group that the dimensions of health that we focused on this week were:
  - Physical
  - Intellectual/Mental
  - Emotional
  - Social

- Vocational
- Spiritual
- If you have adequate time, consider dividing attendees into smaller groups or partners. Assign each group a dimension and ask them to develop descriptors or characteristics of each dimension. Follow up with asking them to discuss how the dimension they are assigned interacts with and is related to the other dimensions. For example, characteristics of vocational health might include a safe and rewarding work environment, positive (or negative) relationships with colleagues, a job that allows the individual to feel that they are contributing to the well-being of others, and a workplace that is intellectually stimulating. How do these characteristics of vocational health fit into the other dimensions?
  - A safe work environment is necessary to protect the physical wellbeing of the individual.
  - A job that is challenging mentally, but not overwhelming, is intellectually stimulating.
  - We often socialize with our colleagues away from work. We have social and emotional connections with our coworkers. These can be both positive and negative interactions.
  - A job that is rewarding and allows us to feel that we are fulfilling our purpose in life builds our self-esteem (social, emotional, mental).
  - For spiritual connection, we may pray for our colleagues or those we meet through our jobs. We may be blessed with a job that allows us to serve others (as Jesus calls us to do).
- As time allows, groups can share a summary of their discussion.
- Please read Acts 20:22–24. Ask the group the following questions for discussion: Did Paul struggle with knowing his vocation (his purpose)? What was Paul's primary purpose? What can we learn from his example? Do you feel God is calling you to a

specific purpose? Is there something in particular God is nudging you to do right now?

- Please read John 4:27–38. Again, food is used as a powerful metaphor—symbolizing something far more important than just filling our tummies. Is God calling you to "reap a harvest?"
- On the reflection page for this week, participants were asked to analyze how they are doing in each dimension of health. Ask if anyone wishes to share or discuss a particular aspect. This could also be a small group activity so that everyone can have an opportunity to share.
- Remind the group that this is a "journey toward wellness." Small changes and a dose of perseverance are our goals. Please be encouraging of small steps toward a healthier lifestyle.
- Ask for questions, comments, or prayer requests.
- Close with prayer.

Additional Review for Brain Health

The same healthful habits that are good for our heart are good for our brain. These include:

- Regular exercise, particularly aerobic (gets our heart rate up and our blood flowing).
- Staying socially and intellectually active.
- Eating a healthy diet.
- Getting adequate sleep.
- Keeping the heart healthy with a healthy lifestyle to avoid chronic diseases.

WEEK EIGHT: WE ARE SANCTIFIED SUGGESTIONS FOR THE LEADER

- Welcome and prayer.
- Read 1 Thessalonians 4:7 and remind group that God did not call us to be impure but to live a holy life.
- When I piloted the study, I showed a great film, *Forks over Knives* (more information on www.forksoverknives.com) at the end of Week Eight. This video illustrates so much of what we discuss during the first seven weeks of the study:
  - The connection between an unhealthy lifestyle and chronic diseases
  - The long-term dangers of obesity
  - The health benefits of a plant-based diet
  - The benefits of regular exercise
  - Real stories of individuals who have changed their lifestyle and have seen dramatic improvements in their health
- It seemed appropriate to me to have this video as a follow-up to a week of focus on Sanctification.

- Review that the Greek word *hagiasmos* is often used interchangeably in the New Testament to mean *holiness* and *sanctified.* It means to reflect what God is—to be clean and pure. Objects or people are sanctified or holy when they are set apart to be used for God's purpose.

- Review with the group that if we are set apart for God's purpose—if we are clean and pure, holy and sanctified, with our body as a temple of the Holy Spirit—shouldn't that body be as healthy as we can possibly make it? That means we need to be very much aware of how we care for our body—what we eat, whether we get adequate exercise, avoiding risky health behaviors, getting adequate rest and relaxation, coping with stress, developing good relationships with others, etc. The list goes on and on.

- If you are unable to obtain a copy of *Forks Over Knives* or if you prefer to have another activity for Week Eight, please feel free to develop an alternative plan.

WEEK NINE: BE A LIGHT SUGGESTIONS FOR THE LEADER

- Welcome and prayer.
- Share an appropriate devotional.
- Review the key points of the meaning of sanctification from the previous week's suggestions. Please ask individual participants to read aloud some or all of the following scriptures:
  - 2 Thessalonians 2:13–16
  - John 17:15–19
  - John 17:20–21
  - Romans 15:14–16
- Ask the group: How does it make you feel to be sanctified? What should be our response? Encourage discussion. Lead group into a focus on service.
- Please share some or all of the following scriptures:
  - 2 Corinthians 4:5–6
  - 2 Corinthians 4:7–10
  - 2 Corinthians 8:7

- ▪ 2 Corinthians 9:6–15
- Ask participants to share some of the gifts they listed on Day 3 of this week (don't accept that they have no gifts).
- On Day 4, participants were asked to list some needs in their church, community, or elsewhere. Ask them to share some of these needs.
- Remind the group that Jesus reminds us to let our light shine. Read Matthew 5:14–16. Ask them where they can let their light shine.
- Read 1 John 1:5–7. Ask the group to pray about what God is calling them to do in service to Jesus, so they may let their lights shine in service to Him.
- Close with Romans 8:31–39, a reminder that nothing can separate us from God.
- Take questions, comments, and prayer requests.
- Provide final words of encouragement. Discuss whether the group wishes to have a celebration (healthy food and game night). See the following section for suggestions.
- The group may decide they wish to continue to meet for exercise, encouragement, and prayer.

SUGGESTIONS FOR FINAL CELEBRATION

- Family members are invited.
- Everyone brings a healthy dish to share (bring recipes to share if group desires).
- Welcome guests (family members).
- Prayer.
- Share food and fellowship.
- Entertainment possibilities include:
  - Individuals share their joys and successes
  - Door prizes (each participant can bring one or more door prizes to share)
  - Games (possibilities are wide open!)

I have developed two games that include material directly from various aspects of the Bible study. Either or both can serve as a fun and entertaining review of the material. If you are interested in more information about these games, you may contact me at katherinepasour@gmail.com.

Happy celebration!

Appendix A:
NUTRITION

There are six nutrients the body needs daily:

1. **Protein** builds and repairs body tissues. Each gram of protein supplies four calories. Amino acids are the building blocks of protein. Sources of complete protein include meat, fish, poultry, milk, yogurt, eggs, and soybeans. The body needs twenty amino acids to function properly and can produce eleven of those. The nine not produced by the body are the essential ones that we must get from our diet. We get incomplete protein (some essential amino acids) from whole grains, corn, legumes (dried bean and lentils), nuts, and seeds. A vegetarian diet can provide all the essential amino acids. Approximately 15 percent of our total caloric intake should come from protein.

2. **Carbohydrates** are our main source of energy and have four calories per gram (same as protein). Carbohydrates include sugar, starches, and fiber. Any excess carbohydrates that are not used for energy are stored in the body and converted to fat (which is why we need to be careful with the types of and how many carbs we

eat). We get carbohydrates from vegetables, potatoes, pasta, bread, cereal, rice, bran, popcorn, and fruit. Simple carbs are sugars that enter the bloodstream quickly and provide quick energy. Sugars occur naturally in fruits, honey, and milk. Processed (simple) sugar is added to many foods. We should limit added sugar to less than 10 percent of our daily calories. For a 2,000 calorie a day diet, that's 200 calories of sugar (not very many considering one twelve-ounce soda has 136 calories). Simple sugars provide calories that are often called "empty" calories because there are no other nutrients. Complex carbohydrates are starches and fiber. Starches provide longer-lasting energy and require more energy to digest (an advantage over simple carbs). Fiber keeps our digestive system (gut) healthy by moving food through our system. Fiber is more filling and helps maintain a healthy weight. We should consume 50 to 55 percent of our daily intake of food in the form of carbohydrates.

3. **Fats** provide energy and help the body store and use vitamins. Fat-soluble vitamins are A, D, E, and K. Fats cushion our internal organs (but more cushion than necessary is dangerous, rather than healthy). One gram of fat has nine calories (more than twice protein and carbohydrates). We should consume 30 to 35 percent of our daily intake of food from fats (primarily the healthier, unsaturated fats).

   a) Saturated fat comes from dairy, meat, and poultry. Saturated fat is solid at room temperature and, when consumed by humans, contributes to higher levels of cholesterol in the body. Lowering consumption of saturated fat can reduce cholesterol and reduce the risk of heart disease.

   b) Unsaturated fat comes from plant products and fish. This fat is usually liquid at room temperature. Polyunsaturated fat comes from sunflower, corn, and soybean oils. Monounsaturated fat comes from olive oil and canola oil.

c) Transfatty acids are produced when polyunsaturated oils have been hydrogenated (added hydrogen).

d) Eating saturated fat, trans fat, or any dietary cholesterol increases LDL (low density lipoprotein), which is the bad cholesterol.

4. **Vitamins** are nutrients that help the body use proteins, carbohydrates, and fats. Vitamins are necessary to maintain normal body functions. Fat-soluble vitamins (A, D, E, and K) need fat to dissolve them for use and storage in the body. Water-soluble vitamins (B complex and C) dissolve in water and cannot be stored in the body. We need vitamins each day, and our best source is a healthy diet, not supplements. Supplements may be necessary for children, pregnant women, the elderly, or people with certain health conditions, but most people should eat a well-balanced diet that provides adequate vitamins rather than taking supplements.

5. **Minerals** are nutrients that regulate many chemical reactions in the body. Macro minerals are required in amounts greater than 100 mg (e.g., calcium and sodium). Trace minerals are necessary but require smaller quantities (e.g., iron, potassium, zinc).

a) Iron is a component of hemoglobin. A deficiency of iron can lead to anemia because the body cannot produce enough red blood cells. The person will feel weak and is more susceptible to illness. The best sources of iron are seafood, leafy green vegetables, whole grains, and lean red meats.

b) Calcium is necessary to build strong bones and teeth and maintain bone strength. Calcium is also needed to assist in muscle contraction and blood clotting. Good sources of calcium are milk and other dairy products, leafy green vegetables, cereal, bread, soy products, tofu, dried beans, and nuts.

c) Sodium regulates and maintains the balance of body fluids. Most Americans consume too much sodium. We should eat less than 2,300 mg of sodium per day. The American Heart Association recommends no more than 1,500 mg of sodium per day.

6. **Water** is needed for all body processes, makes up the basis of our blood, is necessary to remove waste, regulates the body temperature, cushions our spinal cord and joints, and carries nutrients to all our body cells. The human body is more than 60 percent water. We should drink six to eight glasses of water a day. Other sources of water include milk, juice, soup, fruits, and vegetables. Soda and other drinks should not be substituted for water. These act as diuretics, which flush water from the body before it can be used for bodily functions.

Appendix B:
STRESS

Stress can come in two forms.

Eustress is a form of positive stress. Examples may include going on a vacation, getting married, receiving a promotion, retiring, etc. These events in themselves are reasons to celebrate, but they can still be stressful. We also experience a form of positive stress that functions to encourage us to take responsibility for our actions. There may be times when we want to turn off the alarm clock and skip work, but we know we have obligations that we must fulfill. This is a type of positive stress that reminds us to do the things we need to in order to take care of our family and participate fully in society.

Distress is negative stress. Sometimes positive stress may turn into negative stress. For example, when a bride and her family are planning a wedding, the financial strain or the pressure to have everything perfect may create distress for all involved. What should be a happy occasion for a family may turn into an emotional roller coaster that makes a crash landing. Major crises such as being fired, going through a divorce, or the death of a loved one obviously cause negative stress. Workplace conflicts, disagreements about family finances, poor communication among family, and countless other events can also cause stress. We can't avoid stress; it's part of life. The key is managing stress and developing coping skills.

Strategies for dealing with stress:

- Be in the Word. Keep your spiritual relationship with God as the forefront of all you do. Have a quiet time to commune with God daily. Getting up earlier in the morning to have our time with God is ideal. It gets the day off to a good start. This time can involve Bible study, devotion reading, journaling, meditation, and most importantly, *prayer!*
- Participate regularly in physical activity. Exercise is an excellent way of managing stress and should be a part of our daily routine. Even when we cannot get the recommended thirty to sixty minutes of physical activity, short walks or exercise breaks can help relieve stress.
- Resolve to have a healthier lifestyle (that's what this Bible study is all about!). When we are healthier overall, it's easier to cope with stress. Avoid tobacco and other drugs. Limit intake of alcohol. Strive for a healthy diet, rich in fresh fruits and vegetables, whole grains, lean meat, and low-fat dairy.
- It's important to have relaxation time every day. Make an appointment to have fun (and keep it). Laughter is a great stress reliever and it's good for us.
- Social engagement and good relationships with family and friends are essential. Keep the lines of communication open. Have family members or friends who you can talk to when you need a listening ear. You're not asking them to fix the problem or eliminate the stress. Just being able to talk through an issue aloud can provide greater insight to a situation while providing an avenue to relieve stress. Keep your relationships at work col-

legial; work as a team rather than a soloist. Schedule recreational and social outings regularly.

- We cannot avoid all stress, but there are times we can pick and choose. If you have an option to avoid a stressful situation, do it! For example, if driving to work at a particular time has very heavy traffic and is likely to make you late, go in a little earlier. Many times, we bring the stress upon ourselves because of poor time management. Some strategies to help in that area include making a list, prioritizing tasks that must be done, completing tasks early, and allowing more time than you believe a task will take to avoid being late. If you are a procrastinator and you find yourself behind on numerous tasks, it's time to change that behavior. Be an initiator and start early.
- Often, we cannot change the stressor, but we can change our attitude. If we cannot avoid the situation, we can decide to face it with a positive mindset. Accept the challenge and meet it with a smile. Avoid whining or complaining about being over-worked or treated unfairly and face the situation head on with cheerful determination.
- Be sure to get enough (good) sleep.
- Some things we cannot change. In those situations, we need to accept the stressor and cope with it using the strategies listed above.

Appendix C:

OBESITY

According to the Centers for Disease Control (CDC), weight that is higher than the healthy weight for one's height is considered overweight or obese. More than 40 percent of adults in the United States are obese. More than 60 percent are considered overweight. These statistics have increased drastically since 1970.

Body mass index (BMI) is one screening tool to assist in determining whether an individual is at a healthy weight. The formula uses height and weight to make this assessment. Your healthcare provider can evaluate your weight, or you can visit the CDC website to calculate your BMI and use the chart to assess whether you fall into the healthy weight range.

The dangers of being overweight or obese are many and may lead to the increased risk of developing any or all of the chronic conditions below:

- Hypertension (high blood pressure
- High LDL (bad) and low HDL (good) cholesterol
- Type 2 diabetes
- Coronary heart disease
- Stroke

- Gallbladder disease
- Osteoarthritis (breakdown of cartilage and bone in a joint)
- Sleep apnea and breathing problems
- Chronic inflammation
- Some cancers (endometrial, breast, colon, kidney, gallbladder, and liver)
- Mental illness and depression
- Body pain and other physical limitation
- Lower quality of life
- Increased risk of death

The most effective method for preventing obesity is eating a healthy diet (rich in fruits and vegetables, whole grains, lean protein, and low-fat dairy while avoiding foods high in fat, sugar, and sodium). Maintaining a regular exercise program is also essential to good health.

Appendix D:

FIBER

Dietary fiber is also called roughage or bulk and is not digested by our bodies. Fiber passes through our stomach, small intestines, and colon and exits the body. If fiber isn't digested like the proteins, carbohydrates, and fats we consume, why should we bother eating it?

Fiber provides many benefits for us.

- Fiber helps us maintain healthy bowel habits (prevents constipation).
- Fiber can help prevent hemorrhoids and diverticular disease.
- Fiber helps us maintain a healthy weight.
- Fiber helps lower cholesterol.
- Fiber lowers our risk of diabetes and heart disease.

We find fiber in plants—mainly in fruits, vegetables, whole grains, and legumes. There are two types of fiber:

- **Soluble fiber**—This type of fiber dissolves in water to form a gel-like material. Soluble fiber can help lower blood cholesterol and glucose levels. Oats, peas, beans, apples, citrus fruits, carrots, barley, and psyllium are good sources of soluble fiber.

- **Insoluble fiber**—This type of fiber promotes the movement of material through your digestive system and increases stool bulk (helps maintain healthy and regular bowel habits). Whole wheat flour, wheat bran, nuts, beans, and vegetables are good sources.

Our daily diet should include whole grain products, fresh fruits and vegetables, beans, peas, other legumes, nuts, and seeds.

We should also attempt to avoid refined and processed foods such as canned fruits and vegetables, pulp-free juices, white breads and pasta, and foods that are not whole grain. Refining and processing eliminates much of the natural fiber in plant food.

Ways to add fiber to your day:

- For breakfast, choose high-fiber cereals with five or more grams of fiber per serving.
- Eat more whole grains. Check your food labels and seek bread, pasta, and rice that has at least two grams of fiber per serving.
- Try to use whole grain flour as part of the flour in your baked goods. Add crushed bran cereal or uncooked oatmeal to muffins, cakes, and cookies.
- Eat more legumes. There are numerous varieties of beans and peas that can be added to soups, salads, dips, salsa, tortillas, or served as the main dish.
- Aim for five servings of fruits and vegetables daily, prepared in a healthy way (not fried).
- Choose healthy snacks like fresh fruit and vegetables, low-fat popcorn, whole grain crackers, or small servings of nuts.

If you haven't been consuming much fiber, add increased amounts slowly, working toward the goal of twenty to thirty grams of fiber each day.[22]

ADDITIONAL RESOURCES

Nutrition Information
- Academy of Nutrition and Dietetics (formerly the American Dietetic Association) link follows: https://www.nal.usda.gov
- www.choosemyplate.gov
- www.fruitsandveggiesmorematters.org
- www.danielplan.com
- www.doctoroz.com
- www.forksoverknives.com

Health-Related Physical Fitness
- www.FitnessZone.com
- www.MyFitnessPal.com
- www.aarp.org/magazine

Wellness in General
- National Institutes of Health
- American Medical Association
- American Heart Association
- Centers for Disease Control and Prevention

- Mayo Clinic
- www.WebMD.com
- www.verywell.com
- www.HelpGuide.org
- www.prevention.com

ENDNOTES

1 Webster's Encyclopedia of Dictionaries.

2 E.E. Carpenter & P.W. Comfort, *Holman Illustrated Bible Dictionary* (Nashville, TN: Holman Bible Publishers, 2003), p. 1159.

3 Howard W. Stone and James O. Duke, *How to Think Theologically*, 2nd ed. (Minneapolis: Fortress Press, 2006), p. 47.

4 Howard W. Stone and James O. Duke, *How to Think Theologically*, 2nd ed. (Minneapolis: Fortress Press, 2006), p. 49.

5 Centers for Disease Control and Prevention (www.cdc.gov/chronicdisease)

6 Centers for Disease Control and Prevention (www.cdc.gov/chronicdisease)

7 Centers for Disease Control and Prevention (www.cdc.gov/chronicdisease)

8 Centers for Disease Control and Prevention (www.cdc.gov/chronicdisease)

9 Centers for Disease Control and Prevention (www.cdc.gov/chronicdisease)

10 Roger Alliman, *Breaking the Self-Centered life: Understanding God's Ways from the Inside Out* (Freeman, SD: Pine Hill Press, Inc., 1992), p.35.

11 *Holman Treasury of Key Bible Terms* (www.logos.com)

12 www.doctoroz.com

13 *Holman Treasury of Key Bible Terms* (www.logos.com)

14 Howard W. Stone and James O. Duke, *How to Think Theologically*, 2nd ed. (Minneapolis: Fortress Press, 2006).

15 When I was a child and young teenager, my parents listened to a radio segment featuring commentator Paul Harvey every day at lunch. Mr. Harvey shared news, his opinions, and stories. A master storyteller, he would engage his audience with a brief, yet tantalizing glimpse of his story, pause us in suspense for a commercial break, and return to tell us "the rest of the story."

16 *Evangelical Dictionary of Biblical Theology* (logos.com)

17 *Lexham Theological Workbook* (logos.com)

18 R.T. Kendall, *Understanding Theology, Vol. 1* (1996).

19 E.E. Carpenter & P.W. Comfort, *Holman Illustrated Bible Dictionary* (Nashville, TN: Holman Bible Publishers, 2003).

20 Oswald Chambers, *My Utmost for His Highest* (Uhrichsville, Ohio: Barbour Publishing, Inc., 1994), July 23 Prayer.

21 Simon Peter Iredale, *Adult Bible Studies, Vol. 25, No. 1.* (Nashville, TN: 2016).

22 Mayo Clinic (https://www.mayoclinic.org)'

A free ebook edition
is available with the
purchase of this book.

To claim your free ebook edition:

1. Visit MorganJamesBOGO.com
2. Sign your name CLEARLY in the space
3. Complete the form and submit a photo of the entire copyright page
4. You or your friend can download the ebook to your preferred device

Morgan James
BOGO™

A **FREE** ebook edition is available for you or a friend with the purchase of this print book.

CLEARLY SIGN YOUR NAME ABOVE

Instructions to claim your free ebook edition:
1. Visit MorganJamesBOGO.com
2. Sign your name CLEARLY in the space above
3. Complete the form and submit a photo of this entire page
4. You or your friend can download the ebook to your preferred device

Print & Digital Together Forever.

Snap a photo   Free ebook   Read anywhere

CPSIA information can be obtained
at www.ICGtesting.com
Printed in the USA
JSHW040640270822
29844JS00001B/9

9 781631 958731